Contents

D1092142

The Girls' Guide to ELVIS

Introduction

"People are going to want to know what you're doing, where you are, what you wear, what you eat—these things are natural or normal." ELVIS PRESLEY (1962)

Why a girls' guide to Elvis?

Because girls *get* Elvis. Always have, always will.

When girls first saw him perform, we reacted by losing all inhibition: screaming, fainting, trying to tear his clothes off. Ed Sullivan reacted by censoring him from the waist down. Whom would you rather have as your guide?

Unlike Mr. Sullivan, girls like Elvis and his pelvis. Always have, always will.

"Finally, somebody who says what I have been screaming about for twenty out of my thirty-two years! Elvis is the hottest, sexiest, coolest man that ever walked the earth."

A GIRL'S E-MAIL TO
WWW.GIRLSGUIDETOELVIS.COM (2001)

The Girls' Guide to Elvis offers a decidedly female take on what makes Elvis great. Unashamedly focusing on sex, style, and gossip, this illustrated handbook emphasizes the things girls care about, including:

Music

Elvis concerts in the 1950s and 1970s were designed to appeal to his female fan base. Even now, twenty-five years after his death, girls (of all ages) are the primary buyers of Presley CDs. We'll go straight to the fans to find out how Elvis became the King of Rock and Roll.

Movies

Elvis personally hated his movies, but we've always loved them.
Recently, the Girls' Guide to Elvis Presley website conducted a
survey asking chicks to pick their
favorite flick. The results might
surprise you: *Blue Hawaii* got the
most votes, followed by *King
Creole, Viva Las Vegas, Jailhouse Rock,*
and *Change of Habit*. A female film
professor will explain why the
Hawaiian love story is the
definitive Presley vehicle.
We'll also discover which
costar from these above-
mentioned films was a
serious threat to Elvis's
bachelorhood. Here's a
clue: it wasn't the one
who played the nun.

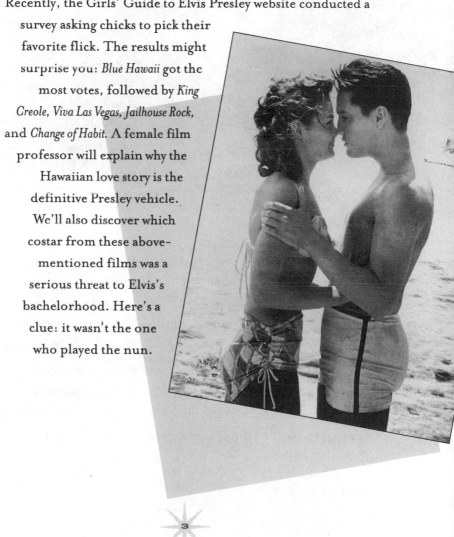

Fashion

Because girls know the true importance of style, we stand in awe of the sideburns, jumpsuits, and Jungle Room. Just think, Elvis did all that without a stylist! As for his coif, only his hairdresser knows for sure, so we'll go directly to the source to find out everything about those jet-black locks. We'll also ferret out the truth about Presley's famous black-leather ensemble (a mistake) and waist-cinching jumpsuits (hint: Saran Wrap has uses outside the kitchen).

Food

Girls empathize with Elvis's lifelong weight issues. Imagine the humiliation of having movie producers write memos about your waistline. If only he had lived to see reduced-fat peanut butter . . . It's too late for Elvis, but not for us. We'll translate his favorite recipes into more diet-friendly options.

Gossip

Stories about manager Colonel Parker, tales from bodyguards, and details about Elvis's prescription drug dependency—girls have heard this rehashed before. We'd rather dish the dirt on his sexual fetishes, unnecessary plastic surgery, and shopaholic binges.

Girls

Check out the harem that accompanied Elvis to his army induction. Girls were often eyewitnesses to key events in the life and career of Elvis Presley. They'll give us special insight into the Elvis phenomenon.

Are you ready for Elvis, girls' style?

Creating the Ultimate Girls' Guide

Although he never wrote an autobiography, Elvis did reveal what he thought and felt at press conferences, in rare personal letters, and onstage. That's where the quotes dotting this book originate.

Girl talk from females who got up close and personal with Presley comes from new interviews and previously published articles, tell-alls, oral biographies, and documentaries.

Old newspapers and magazines were also scanned for illuminating commentary, bizarre theories, and fun facts. Sample tidbit: back in 1968, one male reviewer huffily complained about Elvis's TV special, "I don't think many viewers care to see singers sweat on TV!" Wrong!

For a twenty-first-century perspective, guest "guides" graciously agreed to share their expertise with us in a Q&A format.

Finally, instead of the standard overexposed photos, rare images have been collected from archives and personal collections to provide a unique and intimate perspective: that of girl friends and girl fans.

Just One Last Thing . . .

If you bought this book thinking it was a guide to English singer Elvis Costello, Puerto Rican singer Elvis Crespo, ice-skating star Elvis Stojko, NFL quarterback Elvis Grbac, or *New York Times* film critic Elvis Mitchell, you were sadly misled. Sorry. But did you know that Elvis Presley also sang, skated (albeit roller skating, not ice), played football, and saw a lot of movies? Perhaps there is something in the name.

Chapter 1

Jon Burrows
Wouldn't Smell as Sweet

"Dear Mr. President. First I would like to introduce myself. I'm Elvis Presley . . ."

LETTER TO RICHARD NIXON (1970)

lvis himself complained in 1974, "My little daughter goes around and says, 'Elvis, whatcha you gonna to do?' Swear to God, six years old: 'Elvis!' I say, 'Honey, I'm your daddy, don't call me—' 'Okay, Elvis.'"

Lisa Marie wouldn't have been able to articulate it at such a tender age, but she instinctively knew what all girls know: there's something irresistible about her father's given name. Who would want to say "Daddy" when they can say "Elvis"?

11

Elvis

I Love Elvis. I Hate Elvis. Elvis Is Back. Elvis Now. Elvis Today. This Is Elvis. Elvis Lives. Elvis.com. Elvis! Elvis! Elvis!

The name is magical. Put it on a record, and it will sell. Put it on a movie, no matter how bad, and people will want to see it. On lipstick. On poodle skirts. On dog tags. In big red letters on a television soundstage. In foreign languages for a world-wide satellite broadcast.

Twenty-five years after Elvis's death, it's on things he never even heard of: compact discs, DVDs, and Internet sites. It's even in Microsoft Word's spell check.

Would the whole Elvis thing have happened if his name had been Jon Burrows?

No, the best thing we can say about the name Jon Burrows is it's nondescript. That's why Elvis used it as a pseudonym when traveling. A "Jon Burrows" registered in room 505 at the Washington Hotel? No one looks twice. Except when Mr. Burrows arrives wearing an enormous gold belt, purple suit, and cape.

Presley

For his name we have to thank Rosella Presley, Elvis's great-grandmother.

An unmarried Mississippi sharecropper, Miss Presley had no choice but to give son Jessie her own last name, thus keeping the Presley line going. When Jessie Presley was seventeen, he married the statuesque twenty-five-year-old Minnie Mae Hood. Their son Vernon also married at age seventeen. His bride was twenty-one-year-old Gladys Love Smith. They lied about their ages on the marriage license to make Vernon older and Gladys younger.

On January 8, 1935, in an East Tupelo two-room house built by Vernon, Gladys gave birth to twins. The first baby was delivered stillborn but nevertheless named after Vernon's father. Thirty-five minutes later, the second son was born. This child was given his father's middle name: Elvis.

Before he became famous, the unusual name was often mangled. In a school talent show, it's Prestley. In early concert ads, Ellis and Alvis. In *Billboard*, Pressley.

Aron

Yet Elvis's middle name, Aron, has turned out to be the most problematic. When asked during an army press conference what his middle initial stood for, Pvt. Presley said, "Aron." Aron is on his high school diploma, RCA record contract, and marriage license.

Vernon chose to spell it "Aaron" on his son's grave. The "Elvis Is Alive" brigade cite this as proof that he isn't buried there.

The more traditional and biblical version is what Elvis himself was using at the time of his death. Why? Because he wanted to. He was doing so many crazy things in the 1970s that this late-in-life name change barely registers on the "bizarre" scale.

Regarding the great "Aron" controversy, smart girls sidestep the issue by adopting the "credit card compromise": Elvis A. Presley. If it's good enough for American Express, it's good enough for us!

June 1933—Gladys (age nineteen) and Vernon (age twenty-two) marry.

January 8, 1935—Twins Jesse Garon and Elvis Aron Presley are born.

January 1971—"Aaron" is used on the Jaycees program honoring Elvis as one of America's Ten Outstanding Young Men.

February 1976—Spells his middle name "Aaron" on a police department form he fills out by hand.

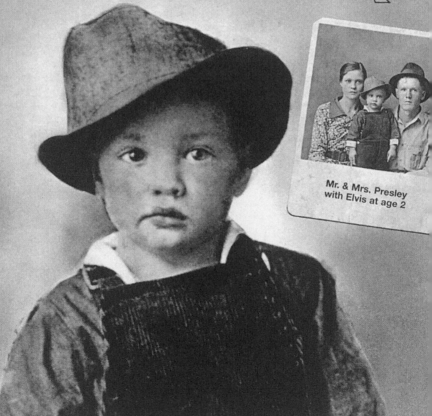

Chapter 2

"I'm 10,000 Years Old"

"ELVIS COUNTRY"

Mr. & Mrs. Presley
with Elvis at age 2

The Little Prince

Q: Did you have a happy time when you were a kid?
EP: All my life I've always had a pretty nice time.
We never had any money or nothing but I
always managed to—I mean, we never had any
luxuries, but we always—we never were hungry,
you know. (1956)

If money hadn't been an issue for the family, Elvis probably would have grown up to marry at age seventeen like his father and grandfather had before him. At twenty-one, instead of having a parade heralding his homecoming appearance at the Mississippi-Alabama Fair and Dairy Show, he probably would have been in his own little Tupelo two-room house, watching his wife change the next generation's diapers.

It took two women to break that cycle. The first is Gladys Presley.

"M" Is for the Million Things She Gave Me

Elvis's mother made countless sacrifices so her son would never have to settle. She thought the world of Elvis, giving him the confidence to be his own person and follow his own interests. Without planning it, she raised him to be the King of Rock and Roll.

For his eleventh birthday, Gladys bought her son his first guitar—even though what Elvis really wanted was a bicycle.

The bike was more than the Presleys could afford. Right beside it in the store's window was a more reasonably priced guitar. "Son, wouldn't you rather have the guitar?" Gladys asked her son. "It would help with your singing, and everyone does enjoy hearing you sing."

Although she did buy him that first guitar, Gladys did not push her son to be a performer. In fact, his career bothered her greatly. She didn't like the traveling, worrying he might have a wreck on the highway or die in a plane crash. True, she was excessively neurotic when it came to Elvis's safety.

But talk to the mothers of Carl Perkins (seriously injured in a 1956 car accident) or Buddy Holly—these fears were completely legitimate.

An Inauspicious Debut

Elvis's first promoter was Mrs. Oleta Grimes, his fifth-grade teacher. Mrs. Grimes thought so highly of his singing at school that she convinced the principal to enter Elvis in the children's talent contest at the Mississippi-Alabama Fair and Dairy Show. Yes, it's the same fair Elvis would later triumphantly headline at age twenty-one.

Elvis sang "Old Shep," a song he would later record on his second album. And? "I won fifth prize," Elvis recalled with a laugh.

Secret Marriage Revealed!

Wouldn't Priscilla be surprised to know she isn't the only Mrs. Elvis Presley? Nor was she the first.

That honor goes to a Tupelo lass, Magdalene Morgan, who also attended the First Assembly of God Church.

In 1948, at the age of thirteen, Elvis made a marriage license for himself and "Magdline." To make it real, he used his parents' marriage license, writing in the blank lines.

Apparently, the Presleys left town before he had a chance to show this document to his "wife." "It was just a very sweet relationship," she clarified years later. "At that time, if you just held hands, it was very serious. And we did hold hands a lot."

Memphis Calls

Where was Vernon in all this?

The senior Presley gave his son many things, including his genes and mannerisms. "Elvis looked a lot like Dad in those days," his mother reminisced while looking at photos of teenage Elvis.

Perhaps the best thing Vernon gave his son was Memphis. The family moved there in 1948. For a teenager with interest in music and movies, Memphis must have seemed like an all-you-can-eat buffet: Beale Street, nightclubs, movie theaters, radio stations, record shops, high-fashion clothing stores, and the Memphis Recording Service (a.k.a. Sun Records).

The only limitation was money. Throughout his high school years, Elvis took on after-school and summer jobs to help support his financially shaky family.

On an employment application form, the female interviewer made the following notation about the high school student: "Rather flashily dressed—'playboy' type denied by the fact he has worked hard past summers. Wants a job dealing with people."

Although the family needed the income from his after-school jobs, Gladys made him quit when it affected his schoolwork.

Prom Date Disaster!

Okay, it really wasn't such a disaster. True, he wore a dark suit when white jackets were the norm.

But the biggest problem was Elvis didn't know how to dance! He and date Regis Wilson were forced to sit around, talking and drinking sodas instead of making their mark on the dance floor.

For a nightcap, Elvis took Regis out for burgers at a local drive-in (at least he had a car!). Regis being only fourteen, Elvis didn't try for anything more than a few kisses. "He was a good kisser," his prom date recalled.

Elvis knew his prom date, Regis, from the neighborhood. They both lived in the same housing project, Lauderdale Courts. Two other Lauderdale Courts sweethearts were

Betty McMahan and Billie Wardlaw. When Billie broke up with him because she wanted to see other boys, Elvis didn't take it well. "Until that night I had never seen a man, or a boy, cry."

Quoted in the *Detroit Free Press* about his teenage love life, Elvis clarified, "I never was a lady killer in high school. I had my share of dates—but that's all."

The Original Goon Boy

Finished with school, Elvis took a job as a truck driver with an electric company, but he almost didn't get the job due to his unusual appearance. The owner's wife, Gladys Tippler, said, "I remember that when she sent Elvis over to see us, the woman at the State Employment Office told me not to judge by appearances. If she hadn't, he'd never have got further than our door, for with that wild hair and those shaggy sideburns, he looked like the original goon boy."

Negative comments about his unorthodox hairstyle and offbeat clothes didn't faze young Elvis. "It really didn't bother him," his father, Vernon, remembered. "He went on like he was anyway."

The Lansky Look

Elvis first discovered the Lansky Brothers store when he was a teenage usher at the Loew's Theater near Beale Street. The flashy, high-fashion clothes were popular with many Beale Street entertainers and appealed to a teenager's taste for out-rageousness.

Bernard Lansky outfitted Elvis in both his junior-senior prom suit coat (pink and black) and rented graduation tuxedo. "After his early records on the Sun label began making him a local hero, all the kids were swarming down to Lansky's on Beale because they wanted pink and black, just like Elvis wore."

It wasn't just the colors. It was the collars, big and high, sometimes rolled up, sometimes velvet. And the pants, pegged or baggy, trimmed with a ribbon down the outside seam. Half boots of patent leather, often white. "He never wore any middle-of-the-road, run-of-the-mill stuff. It was always something spectacular."

When Presley first began performing decked out in prime Lansky gear, the reviewers felt compelled to report on his clothes as well as his singing. "For his appearance on the Hayride, Elvis wore white shoes with blue soles, a green coat, blue pants, and white shirt, tie and silk scarf," noted the *Shreveport Times*.

Elvis continued to patronize Lansky's throughout the sixties and seventies. Lansky even provided the white suit Elvis was buried in.

After a lifetime of dressing Elvis, Bernard Lansky can still recall young Elvis's sizes: 42 coat, 32 waist, 15½ by 34 shirt, 10½ boot. Elvis grew into a 48 coat and 40 waist. Lansky attributed this to years of "good eatin'."

January 1946—Gladys buys Elvis a second-choice gift for his eleventh birthday.

November 1948—The Presleys leave Mississippi for Tennessee.

Fall 1950—Works as a movie usher, begins window shopping at Lansky's.

June 1953—Graduates from Humes High School with a major in shop.

April 1954—Starts driving a truck for Crown Electric.

Chapter **3**

SUNRISEELVISPRESLEY

The Kid with the Sideburns

Q: When you released that first record, did you
think you would have such a successful career
as you have?

EP: No, I don't think anyone did, did we, Mr.
Phillips? (laughs). I don't think so. Nobody
had any idea, really. (1961)

One day, shortly after he got out of high school, Elvis
called his father into his room to announce he wanted
to be an entertainer. This was not like Ricky Nelson telling
Ozzie he wanted to sing on the show. This was a kid on track to
become an electrician telling his often out-of-work father that
he wanted to pursue a pie-in-the-sky dream.

Although Vernon had his doubts ("I never saw a guitar
player that was worth a damn," Elvis remembered him saying),
he knew his son was acquainted with a few local singers. "Why

don't you talk to some of them to see what you got to do to get into it," Vernon counseled.

The Shocking Truth Behind His First Recording Session

How did he go from truck driver to rock and roll star? The publicity machine decided it all started with a record he made for his mother's birthday. At first, Elvis resisted this story the press seemed to want so badly.

When asked point-blank if the record had been a birthday present, Elvis clarified that he made it just to try it, to hear himself sing. Later it became part of Presley lore that Gladys inspired the first visit to Sun.

I Was the First to Record Elvis Presley

Marion Keisker, the girl Friday of Memphis Recording Service/Sun Records, was the first person Elvis dealt with. If there hadn't been a friendly female face to greet him, who knows if the shy teenager would have been brave enough to admit he wanted to make a record.

Marion was so impressed with Elvis that she made an extra taped copy of his session for studio owner Sam Phillips. "I thought, 'Oh, I want Sam to hear this.' Sam's been saying he wanted to find a white man who sounded black, and I felt that was what was happening here. Actually, something more was happening. But that's what I heard, that he sounded black to me."

She continued to promote Presley to Phillips, reminding him about "the kid with the sideburns" when they were discussing potential new singers.

Sideburns?!

Elvis's unusual facial hair was a big deal back then. Shocking in the way Mohawks were in the early days of punk rock. In interview after interview, he was grilled about "this sideburn business." Young Presley always explained that he just liked them, always had, and grew them as soon as he was old enough.

Just Add Scotty and Bill, Mix Thoroughly, Serve Hot

There was no denying Elvis had a look, along with a good feel for ballad singing and a strong sense of rhythm as he banged away on his guitar. Yet he was a singer with no real experience, no repertoire of material, and no band.

Sam Phillips put Elvis together with guitarist Scotty Moore and bassist Bill Black. At the first rehearsal, Scotty's wife, Bobbie, remembers Elvis wearing a white lacy shirt, pink pants with black piping, and white bucks. His hair was "kind of odd for that time." And he had pimples.

In the recording studio, the trio tried out a wide range of songs for Phillips, none of which he felt were worth recording. "Elvis was the only Sun artist who did not have his own material," pointed out Marion Keisker. "All the other artists who came in, Johnny Cash, Roy Orbison, all of them, had scads of their own material. Or in case they didn't have a song that Sam liked, some other artists had it—but it was all new material. Elvis didn't write songs, and we couldn't find one that seemed right for him. Although he had a marvelous ear. You could just sing it once or go through it once, he knew the song and knew what to do with it. It was a matter of weeding it out."

Then, just messing around between "real songs," Elvis and the boys did "That's All Right, Mama."

Everyone in the studio knew they had struck gold.

Later, when asked how he came across this sound, Elvis downplayed it. "I just landed upon it accidentally, more or less."

Thus the first Sun superstar was born.

The Cute Factor

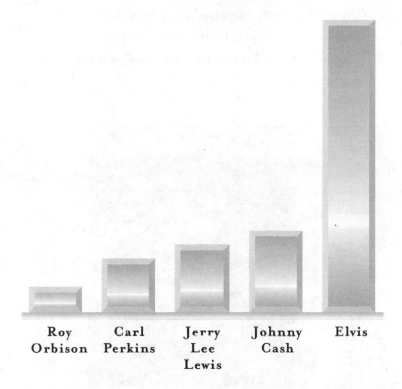

| Roy Orbison | Carl Perkins | Jerry Lee Lewis | Johnny Cash | Elvis |

After Elvis blasted the doors wide open, Sun quickly established an amazing stable of young rock and roll singers making hit records. However, there was one crucial difference that Sam Phillips must not have taken into account when he sold Elvis's contract to RCA and bet on Carl "Blue Suede Shoes" Perkins. A certain something that any girl could have told him was essential: the cute factor. With a little polishing, Elvis was unbeatable. The best the others could hope for on a really good day was "moderately handsome."

Credit to the cute-impaired, they didn't hold Elvis's success against him. You hear their real camaraderie on *The Million Dollar Quartet*, which took place after Elvis was already a big recording star for RCA.

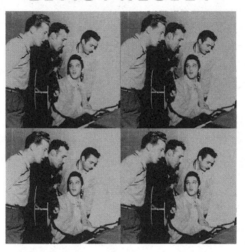

ELVIS PRESLEY

The Million Dollar Quartet

Mid-1953—Makes his first "personal recording" at Sun almost immediately after finishing high school.

July 8, 1954—First official Sun song, "That's All Right, Mama," is played on influential Memphis radio show *Red, Hot and Blue.*

July 27, 1954—Marion Keisker accompanies Elvis to his very first newspaper interview. "This boy has something that seems to appeal to everybody," she tells the reporter.

Chapter

"Girls,
I'll See You Backstage"

Q: Your actions make quite a reaction in the audience. What is your opinion of the audience?

EP: Well, I mean it would look pretty funny out there without one. Actually, I suppose you're talking about all the yelling and everything. Actually, it's good because it covers up my mistakes, you see. Whenever I hit a sour note, well nobody knows it but me. (1957)

Before 1956, Elvis was put on concert rosters as a supporting act. In theory, this made sense. He had only a few singles out on the tiny Sun label. Quite often no one knew who he was before he went onstage.

They never forgot him after.

Part of it was the way he looked. Part of it was the way he

sounded. Mostly it was the way he performed—the intensity, the showmanship, the animal magnetism, the teasing, the gyrations, and the sex appeal. Sometimes he refused to move for minutes on end, just to get a reaction. To the future King of Rock and Roll, a show was a failure unless the crowd went absolutely wild.

It was all so radically different from the acts that came before. Most performers just stood still and sang. Very bland, very tame. Think Pat Boone. Elvis and his gyrations were exciting. Thrilling. Girls recognized right away that Elvis Presley was the hottest thing going.

"I Like Him Because . . ."

Girls projected their fantasies onto the singing star, preferring to imagine him as a dangerous, illicit creature instead of the friendly, polite young man that he was in real life.

Newsweek asked female concertgoers in Texas what the appeal was. "I like him because he looks so mean." "He's fascinating—like a snake." "I hear he peddles dope."

"He's just a great, big, beautiful hunk of forbidden fruit," a Florida girl weighed in. "We think he's the absolute end," another girl wrote in to *Life* magazine. "He just makes me feel so crazy!" declared a San Antonio fan.

The questions of a Daytona high school girl interviewing Elvis backstage reveal typical points of fascination: "Do you like the girls going wild over you?" Presley answered, "That's what keeps me in business." "I have another one, I don't know if I should ask it or not. Um, are you a dope fiend?" "Yes," Elvis joked with a laugh.

I Was the First Elvis Impersonator

One girl even went as far as imitating Elvis in her school talent show. "After seeing him in person many times and drawing him countless times in my notebooks, I discovered that I could put make-up on to look like Elvis," said ninth-grader Nancy Hebenstreit. "I thickened and shaped my eyebrows, fattened my lips and added side-burns." Her act elicited a response very similar to Elvis's: girls squealed and the principal told her she couldn't "move like that" if she wanted to be part of the second scheduled performance.

I Started Elvis's First Fan Club

Kay Wheeler founded the nation's first and largest Elvis Presley fan club in 1955. She was fifteen.

One Saturday afternoon Kay was hanging out at a radio station where her aunt worked when a disc jockey came in with an Elvis single and said it was the worst thing he'd ever heard.

A typical rabid teenage fan, Kay defended Elvis, blurting out a spontaneous claim that "I even have a fan club for him!" It wasn't really a lie—she and her sister were fans.

"He looked at me like I was crazy," Kay recalled. "Apparently, he came back, asked my aunt for my address, and as a joke, played that record on the air, announcing that if anybody wanted to join the fan club for this idiot, write Kay Wheeler." Kay only knew this had happened when several hundred letters arrived on her doorstep.

The First Riot

Q: When you get caught in a mob, have you ever
been seriously hurt by the girls?

EP: Yes, I've been scratched and bitten and
everything.

Q: What do you think about it?

EP: I just accept it with a broad mind because

actually they don't intend to hurt you. I mean, it's not that. They want pieces of you for souvenirs, is all. (1957)

The first riot occurred in Florida. Mae Axton, the local promoter recalled, "Elvis closed the first half, while the show's star closed the second half. As Elvis finished his set, he said, 'Thank you, ladies and gentlemen. And girls, I'll see you backstage.' I'd say half of the 14,000 there jumped up and started for the stairs that led to the ballplayers' dressing room, which was 'backstage.' It was like a sudden ocean swell."

Headlining acts quickly learned that they didn't want to follow Elvis.

I Wrote Elvis's First Big Hit

Mae Axton wasn't only a concert promoter. She also wrote the first Elvis Presley single that went gold.

"I told Elvis when he started talking to Colonel Tom Parker that all he needed was a man like Colonel Tom at the helm and a million-dollar song. I facetiously said, 'I'll write your first million seller, you continue to be you, and Colonel Tom will do the rest.' And so it was that one of my song writing collaborators, Tommy Durden, came over and showed me a story in the paper about a man who had rid himself of all identity, written a one-line sentence, 'I walk a lonely street,' and killed himself." Inspired, Mae and Tommy wrote "Heartbreak Hotel."

Mid-July 1954—First live appearance at a local club in Memphis.

May 1955—Causes a riot in Florida.

October 1955—Kay Wheeler writes to Presley's manager to inform him of her newly minted fan club. Secretary Carolyn Asmus responds that since Presley is just one out of the full list of acts Parker handles, and since there are no existing organizations and no plans to start one,

"Colonel Tom Parker has advised me to tell you to 'do anything you want to in regard to forming a fan club for Elvis Presley.' "

January 1956—Records Mae Axton's "Heartbreak Hotel."

January 1956—Performs for the last time as a supporting act.

October 1956—The first Elvis impersonator takes the stage—in the form of a teenage girl in her father's oversized jacket, lipsynching to "Heartbreak Hotel."

Chapter **5**

A Date with Elvis

"I love going out on dates, especially with a girl that likes to have fun. The kind of fun I mean is just going out, looking around at places and things, wondering about people. Trying to win prizes in the amusement park. And just generally having a good time." ELVIS PRESLEY (1956)

Although Elvis always proclaimed that he never thought of himself as a "lady-killer," he was more than willing to date the young women who came across his path. And he didn't limit the fun to just one girl. A date with the burgeoning rock star often included all of his friends and anyone else who wanted to tag along. It wasn't unusual to find girls napping in their car parked outside Graceland's gates, exhausted after roller skating late at night with Elvis at the Rainbow Roller-dome.

Dinner and a Movie, Elvis Style

Even when he was dirt poor, Elvis would scratch up enough money to take a date to the movies. When he became famous, he made arrangements with the Memphian Theatre for private after-hours screenings.

Barbara Glidewell complained about going to the movies with Elvis, "You thought maybe it was going to be just a few people, but he would invite the whole world. And you just didn't want to share him."

His date would sit next to him, and everyone else in his party would sit behind. Fans who tracked him down at the theater were allowed in as his guests. Everything—including popcorn, candy, and soda from the snack counter—was free. Seventies-era girlfriend Linda Thompson first met Elvis at one of these screenings.

Step Right Up, Win a Prize!

Elvis grew up going to the fair. In Memphis, there was an actual amusement park, which Presley would rent out for midnight fun. Fifties steady Anita Wood was a frequent partner in bumper car and roller coaster madness.

When Elvis performed in Las Vegas for the first time in 1956, teenage fan Nancy Hebenstreit encountered him killing time at a penny arcade. Nancy recalled, "It was the middle of the day in the middle of the week, and there was no one else there except ELVIS!" Among the highlights of their impromptu date: messing around in a twenty-five-cent photo booth. Pictures of the two of them together were ripped up by Nancy's jealous boyfriend, but one of Elvis survived.

Come to My House

A fan once asked, "Why do you always take beautiful girls to Memphis to meet your folks when you have no intention of marrying these girls?" Elvis replied, "My folks always like to know my friends and the girls I date . . . and I like them to."

Once he started making motion pictures, Elvis invited actresses to visit Memphis. Natalie Wood came in 1956, Yvonne Lime in 1957. Vegas showgirls were also brought back home, including Marilyn Evans and Sahara dancer Dottie Harmony, who spent Christmas with the Presleys.

Dottie Harmony stayed in Elvis's pink-and-white bedroom, while Elvis camped out in the playroom. It was all very innocent. "I'm not kidding. We read the Bible aloud together."

Elvis Presley, Tour Guide

Elvis loved to drive people around his beloved adopted city. One such tour resulted in one of the most amazing Elvis records ever released, *The Million Dollar Quartet*. One night in December 1956, Elvis was driving around Memphis with visiting Las Vegas showgirl Marilyn Evans. Sun Records was on the "Elvis tour," so they dropped in to say hello and stayed to jam awhile. That's Marilyn posed on the piano.

The Girl He Almost Married

Elvis admitted, "I suppose the closest that I ever came to getting married was just before I started singing—in fact, my first record saved my neck."

Dixie Locke was fifteen when she first met nineteen-year-old Elvis. Their romance was all very 1950s. They first spoke to each other at the roller rink. When they became serious, she wore his class ring. He took her to her junior prom.

Doesn't Elvis look much spiffier than he did at his own prom!

With Dixie, Elvis established a pattern that he would expect all future serious girlfriends to follow. While he was off on tour, his official girlfriend was expected to sit quietly at home, preferably his home, keeping his mother company. He'd get unreasonably jealous if he even thought she was seeing some other boy behind his back. Of course, what he did on the road with other girls didn't count.

Ultimately, Dixie had enough and found another boy to fall in love with. Another pattern: even when it was obvious that the relationship was over, Elvis would let it limp on rather than initiate a breakup.

Although you'd think, "How could a girl snag someone better than Elvis Presley?" most girls did! They found guys ready to get married—and stay married. Interestingly, the men often had professional skills that Elvis himself would consider superior. Steady Anita Wood would marry a pro football player, wife Priscilla would run away with a karate master, and longtime girlfriend Linda Thompson settled down first with a celebrated Olympic athlete and then a high-powered record producer.

By early 1957, Dixie would be married to someone else, while Elvis waited ten more years before he tied the knot.

May 1955—Leaves a concert tour to attend Dixie's prom.

May 1956—Messes around at the Last Frontier Village during the day while appearing in Las Vegas for the first time.

October 1956—Steps out with James Dean's *Rebel Without a Cause* girlfriend, Natalie Wood.

November 1956—Vacations in Las Vegas. Discovers a liking for showgirls. Dates dancer Dottie Harmony. Meets Marilyn Evans.

December 1956—Shows Marilyn Evans Memphis. Introduces her to his pals at Sun Records.

Solid Gold

Q: Do you call it singing—the stuff you do?
EP: Do I call it singing?
Q: Yeah, that is what you call it, right?
EP: Well, I've sold five million records, somebody
    calls it singing (laughs). (1956)

The Presley phenomenon went national when RCA Victor bought his recording contract from Sun Records for what was then considered to be an out-of-the-ballpark figure of $40,000. It's the equivalent of Hollywood nowadays paying movie stars $20 million a picture. RCA's investment is even more astronomical when you consider that everyone, including Elvis, thought rock and roll might not last.

Keep Me Always on Your Lips

What does Elvis Presley have in common with Wyatt Earp, the Lone Ranger, and Lassie? In 1956, after appearances on Ed Sullivan and other variety shows, he too was a TV phenomenon. The same man who marketed the cowboy and dog merchandise took on the King of Rock and Roll. Of course, Elvis's fan base was skewed more toward females. Adjustments were made.

Among the fabulous products marketed to us girls:

Hound Dog Orange nonsmear lipstick—"Keep me always on your lips!"

Elvis brooch—"Wear his signature close to your heart!"

The Elvis Presley Doll—"He'll be your companion— morning, noon, and night time, too!"

Newsweek reported that 450,000 one-dollar lipsticks, 350,000 charm bracelets (also priced at $1), and 80,000 pairs of jeans ($2.98 a pair) were sold.

Look magazine sneered at the merchandising blitz in November 1956: "It's hard to believe that the teenage girls of the land could carry that much dough in the pockets of their green-stitched black-denim Elvis Presley jeans, but they are the ones who make the Presley Industry pay off. There must be a couple of million awkward, unjelled American females who, in the next five years or so, will be reasonably intelligent American women. But today, an appalling number of them insist on knowing nearly all the details of Elvis Presley's life and times and make a great nuisance of themselves playing Presley records at home and squealing at his concerts. If you are troubled by all this, you needn't be; they will get over it. Some day, they will all yawn at once when Elvis comes bleating out of the loud speaker. They will lay away the green-stitched jeans, the sneakers, bobby sox, T-shirts and funny hats with the Presley imprimatur. They'll lose the Presley charm bracelets for which they paid a dollar, and the two-dollar plaster-of-Paris Presley busts will be covered with dust."

Or not. Twenty-five years after his death, Elvis's estate still earns an estimated $35 million a year—a large part from merchandising.

Hollywood Calls

Q: Did they tell you at the studio that they thought
you were a good actor?

EP: Well, uh, no, they didn't say they thought I was
good, they just told me that my test turned out
real well. (1956)

Although Elvis was an
ultracontemporary
singing sensation, he
made his film debut in a
Civil War—era drama,
playing the youngest
Reno brother in a film
called *The Reno Brothers*
(quickly renamed *Love
Me Tender* after Elvis's
hit song). This was
the first and only
time Elvis did not
receive top billing.

When the motion
picture was released in
November 1956, it was
clear to one and all that
girls weren't piling
into the theaters for
stars Richard Egan
and Debra Paget.

Gilded Elvis

As 1957 began, the whirlwind showed no sign of stopping.
Movies, concerts, records, and even Elvis himself continued

to get bigger and better.

His naturally sandy hair
was dyed black, acne-prone
skin treated, teeth capped,
and small flaws corrected.
His cousin Billy Smith said,
"Nobody teased him about
getting all dandified because

his teeth looked so good before that it was hard to tell the difference, except for the whiteness. And for a little gap he had. He also had the warts removed from his hands."

Now instead of off-the-rack apparel, Elvis performed in a customized suit that was so outrageous it became a symbol of rock and roll.

The Golden Idol

Although gaudy was never a problem for Elvis, even he thought the gold suit a little much.

"The Colonel asked for something spectacular, and my grandfather came up with the idea," explained Jamie Mendoza, granddaughter of the suit's designer, Nudie.

Elvis's manager was a friend of the famous costumer, who had created many of Hank Williams's stage outfits (and would also design the *Loving You* red satin cowboy gear and the *Clambake* baseball-stitched suit).

Nudie also had a good understanding of the Elvis phenomenon,

thanks to his daughter Barbara. Here she is pictured with the
teen idol.

Presley gamely
wore the full Nudie
suit twice in concert.
When he slid on his
knees, he left gold
streaks. As a
compromise, he
wore the coat
but matched it
with basic
black pants.
"Hysterical
Shrieks Greet
Elvis in His
Gold Jacket
and Shoes,"
blared the
headline of
a 1957 concert review.

The golden coat was such a big part of his concert persona
that he dug it out again when he came back from the army and
performed the Pearl Harbor benefit show in 1961.

March 1956—First long-playing album released. By May, it will be the biggest-selling album in RCA's history. Flies to Hollywood to take a screen test.

April 1956—First gold record—"Heartbreak Hotel"—as Mae Axton prophesized.

August 1956—Begins shooting his first motion picture.

November 1956—*Love Me Tender* opens.

December 29, 1956—Makes *Billboard* history by having ten songs in the Top 100.

January 6, 1957—"From the waist up" Sullivan show.

January 1957—Dyes his hair black for *Loving You.*

March 1957—Wears the gold suit for the first time at a concert in Chicago.

Chapter 7

There's No Place Like Home

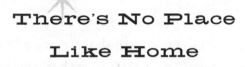

Q: Elvis, where do you live at home in Memphis?

EP: Where do I live at home? I live at home! (laughs).

Q: No, I mean do you have your own house or apartment?

EP: Ah yes, we have a house in Memphis.

Q: You and your parents?

EP: Yes. (1956)

"You got to give Elvis credit," a fan magazine stated in 1956. "First thing he did when he made a hit was to get a nice home for his family."

In Tupelo, the Presleys moved around a lot depending on their financial standing. The same was true in Memphis. It wasn't until Elvis started making money that they could afford to buy a house and really make a home.

The house he bought in March of 1956 was on Audubon Drive, in a new, upscale, exclusive section of Memphis. When asked about the new house, Elvis described it as "a ranch-type, seven-room house. Three bedrooms, a den, playroom. It's a pretty nice place."

Used to inhabiting two-room apartments, the Presleys had a lot of shopping to do to furnish their new home. His bemused mother reported, "Elvis is always buying something for the house when he's out on one of his trips. His latest is lamps. He's brought me so many lamps that I have to put some of them away and take turns using them. If ever there was a boy who cares about his home, it's Elvis."

I Live in Elvis's House

Cindy Hazen, who with her husband, Mike Freeman, has written *Memphis Elvis-Style,* currently resides in the Presleys' Audubon Drive house. She is our guest expert guide.

GG2E: Tell us everything!

CH: Well, Elvis bought this house in 1956. It was a very new neighborhood then, kind of on the outskirts of the city. Very, very swanky neighborhood. Lots of doctors and lawyers, those sorts of people.

Coincidentally, Sam Phillips did not live too far away—within a couple of miles. My guess is that's how Elvis became aware of this area and neighborhood.

The Presleys lived here for thirteen months. As his fame increased, there was no privacy at this location. That's when they ended up getting Graceland. But I believe that until everything became so chaotic he fully intended to stay on Audubon Drive.

He did so much to the house during the period of time that he was here. He added the pool. In December of 1956, he added a six-hundred-square-foot game room and another bathroom. They planted trees in the front— huge trees. That's not something anyone who intended to leave would have done.

GG2E: What is specifically "Elvis" about the house?

CH: The game room has two trophy cases, one on either side. Very large trophy cases. He had those built because he was getting so many awards that year.

The bathroom that he added in the back is very, very Elvis. The color is Ming green. It's got the green toilet, green sink, and green formica with swirls. On the wall there are all these mirrors. I mean, it's just so Elvis.

We've also uncovered some wallpaper in the hallway that's absolutely wonderful. It's turquoise and black and gold—with musical notes and piano keys!

A lot of the decorating things he did at Graceland he started doing at this house. The mirrors, for example. Certainly the brick and wrought-iron fence, that's something he later did at Graceland.

Why Kings' Castles Have Moats

"At the time they purchased it," a fan magazine reported about the Audubon house, "certain socialites in the vicinity had rude things to say about 'that loud, that awful singer.' "

They soon discovered it wasn't Presley that was the problem—it was his fans. The house was too accessible. It didn't matter that Elvis was off on tour most of the time, people would hang out anyway. Girls would pick blades of grass or wipe dust off the cars as souvenirs.

Elvis didn't mind, but the neighbors did. There's a famous story, which may be apocryphal, that they tried to buy him out.

In any event, the Presleys were outgrowing the place. Elvis complained that a song written for him was sent over to the house, and he never even saw it because there was so much junk everywhere.

Graceland, Home to the King of Rock and Roll

Virginia Grant got Elvis Graceland. Ms. Grant was a real estate agent who was hired by Gladys Presley after casually meeting one day at a department store. Hearing that the Presleys were interested in a Colonial home, Ms. Grant immediately showed them Graceland.

"I think I'm going to like this new home," Gladys told reporters. "We will have a lot more privacy and a lot more room to put some of the things we have accumulated over the last few years."

As with the Audubon house, Elvis was the second owner of Graceland. A family named Moore originally built it in 1939. The name "Graceland" was established before the house was even built. It originally referred to the five-hundred-acre farmland owned by the Toof family (daughter Grace Toof inspired the distinctive nomenclature).

Elvis bought Graceland in March of 1957 for $100,000. He immediately began customizing the house and continued to do so throughout his life.

The first order of business was setting up a clear demarcation of "inside" and "outside." Elvis added the surrounding wall made out of pink Alabama fieldstone and the iron door "music" gates in 1957.

Fans were welcome to hang out at Graceland—down by the gates. Elvis would come down to see them.

Elvis Presley, Interior Decorator Nonpareil

Inside Graceland, Elvis could do anything he wanted.

As a decorator, he played by his own rules. Carpeting on the ceiling? Sure! Put it on the doors while you're at it. Like to watch TV in bed? Go for broke with a 9' × 9' double king-size bed with two television sets recessed in the ceiling directly above. Isn't it a pain the way you have to turn on a light to look in the closet? Why can't they be rigged like refrigerator lights? At Graceland, they can! Got a personal logo? Paint it on the wall. Who's going to stop you? You can always change it later if you don't like it. That's what makes Graceland so fabulous. Anything goes.

Q: There was one story that said you might sell
Graceland. Is that true?

EP: That's strictly a rumor. I would never sell
Graceland. Not at no price to nobody, as long as
I can hang on to it. Besides, it would be foolish
to sell now that I've got it completed. (1959)

When Elvis was alive, only invited guests saw the interior of Graceland. Since 1982, Graceland has been open to one and all as a tourist attraction. The estate estimates 600,000 people visit Elvis's beloved home each year. For those who can't attend in person, the official website, www.elvis.com, offers a virtual tour.

Making Sense of Graceland

Our guest girl guide to Graceland is Karal Ann Marling, professor of art history and American studies at the University of Minnesota and author of *Graceland: Going Home with Elvis*, published by Harvard University Press.

GG2E: Why does Graceland hold such particular fascination for girls in particular?

KAM: It's akin to the feeling that you get when you go into somebody else's house—it's fascinating to see what's there and how it's been put together. And with Elvis, it's a man who did all this arranging!

Over the years he had himself photographed in his house to capture various moods, which is something we all do. We arrange our houses to be the perfect environments in which to present ourselves. And Elvis was very self-conscious about that. He used to give interviews to the press just about his home decorating plans. You don't often hear Harrison Ford or Mick Jagger giving lengthy interviews to the press about what color they intend to paint the ceiling in their entrance hall.

GG2E: Why was Elvis so focused on things like that?

KAM: It's a complicated issue. Partly, I think, it had to do with the house he was born in. He used to go down there in his car, take absolutely baffled friends with him, and they would just sit outside of that little house in Tupelo, Mississippi. The house was sort of a symbol to him of where he started and what he was going to be better than. As a grown-up, when people came to visit him, especially from Tupelo, he would always say, "You know you could fit that little house I was born in in the music room in this house two times and have room left over." So it was a measuring device in a way.

Also, because Graceland was a classical *Gone with the Wind* Southern mansion with the big columns in the front, it was a symbol of his own personal identity. He didn't leave the South. He didn't move to Hollywood. He had houses there, but the place he identified with most strongly was the place of his birth, the South. The house is a symbol of that.

GG2E: How would you describe Elvis as an interior decorator?

KAM: It's hard to categorize it. It's middle-class taste, certainly. Elvis was not a member of the middle class, so to him that was aspiring upward.

It's middle-class taste carried to an extreme degree. Where there are big chairs in somebody's house, his were going to be the biggest chairs in the universe.

The basic lines of things didn't diverge that much from the common taste, but the dimensions, the proportions, and above all the colors! There's nothing timid about the color.

GG2E: What about each room having a different theme? It's almost Disneyland-like.

KAM: Yes, there's certainly a bit of that theming, but part of that might be because Priscilla redecorated the dining room and living room before it was open to the public. The way we see it now, it's a little more like a hotel lobby. It's more conventionally tasteful than Elvis himself preferred it.

GG2E: What are five things girls shouldn't miss when touring Graceland?

KAM: One of the things to see in his father's office is one of the original lamps that Elvis used to buy for his parents when he was out on the road in

the pre-Graceland days. It's this absolutely
fabulous Jetsons lamp from the 1950s. That's
a do-not-miss.

Another thing you don't want to miss is the
Jungle Room, of course. Elvis didn't mean to
have it that way forever. He died before it got
redecorated. But it was a kind of exuberant joke
to him. It would be like if your mother gave you
$200, said that you could do your room over
from Target, and you just ran out and bought all
the absolutely coolest stuff you could possibly
buy. That's what the Jungle Room is all about.

A third thing is the façade of the house.
The perfect portico with the big white columns.
Then, if you stand there and look down the
street, what do you see but a Krispe Kreme
doughnut shop and a barbecue place! He chose
to live in this house which was no longer really
out in the country but in the heart of what we
would nowadays call a commercial strip.

In fact, the house was a sort of advertisement
of himself. The house is up on a hill with this
elaborate metal fence. He lit the façade up.
It's like a giant billboard.

A fourth thing to see at Graceland is Elvis's
collection of cars. If he bought them in one
color, he was apt the next day to have them
painted another color. He once went to a car
dealership, squeezed a bunch of grapes on the
hood of a Cadillac, and said he wanted it exactly
that color.

If I had to pick one last thing to look at in
Graceland, I might pick his sofa in the living
room. Because it looks just like the sofa in your
living room or my living room—nothing
unusual about it at all except it's about four
times as long! His sentiments are just like ours
but bigger, written larger than life.

March 1956—Moves into the Audubon Drive house. Purchases it outright for $30,000 and will sell it a year later for $55,000.

March 1957—Buys Graceland for $100,000.

January 1972—Part of Highway 51 South is renamed after Elvis. Graceland's street address becomes 3764 Elvis Presley Boulevard.

June 1982—Graceland opens to the public as a tourist attraction.

1991—The King of Rock and Roll's house is officially listed on the National Register of Historic Places.

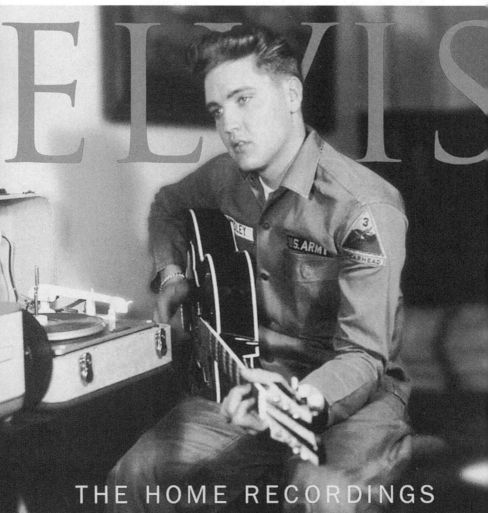

ELVIS

THE HOME RECORDINGS

Soldier Boy

"Well, I gotta go wade in the mud."

ELVIS PRESLEY, LETTER FROM GERMANY
TO A FRIEND BACK HOME (1958)

Elvis was at the peak of his career when Uncle Sam called. Other than a request to make one last motion picture before induction, Elvis tried to play it straight as he became Pvt. Elvis Presley, serial number 53310761.

Of course, not many other GIs had their induction covered by the worldwide press and their dog tags duplicated as souvenirs for their female fan base. Nor did they receive fifteen thousand letters per week during mail call.

Deep in the Heart of Texas

Basic training took place at Fort Hood, an open base, which meant that anyone could drive right on. Local high school girls like Jane Levy Christie drove around on the weekends, looking for the famous soldier. "Once, we found him and took him for a ride to the Dairy Queen, which our boyfriends didn't like very much."

Memphis girlfriend Anita Wood went to visit him in Texas. "Elvis looked tanned and wonderful. He had no dye on his hair, it was not a crewcut but it was cut short, he looked great."

But . . . "We couldn't go anywhere, even on the post, without him being mobbed. Really, those boys were just as bad as the girls ever are about Elvis. If he went to the PX or the movies, they would mob him every time. About the only place we could go without a whole lot of people crowding around was one of the Snow Queen ice places at the edge of the post."

To achieve some semblance of normalcy, Elvis imported his parents, grandmother, and a friend or two to live with him off-base in nearby Killeen. Neighbors immediately complained about the resulting hullabaloo.

A Time of Grief

While in Texas, Gladys Presley became seriously ill. Her doctor recommended returning to Memphis. Elvis was granted emergency leave when his mother was hospitalized. After a bedside visit, Gladys sent him back to Graceland to rest. Only her husband was with her when she died.

Elvis was devastated by the loss, but the regimented army life turned out to be a blessing in disguise. He reflected much later, "It was a time of grief for me. My mother had just died and I had to leave my home and go to Germany. It came at a time when I sorely needed a change. God's hand at work. The army took me away from myself and gave me something different."

In Germany, "something different" arrived in the form of a fourteen-year-old American schoolgirl whose father was stationed nearby. Her name was Priscilla Beaulieu. She fascinated the twenty-four-year-old soldier.

"I met him at a very vulnerable time, just after the death of his mother," said Priscilla. "So I met a different Elvis, an Elvis who was grieving, very lonely. I didn't get the sense of him being a movie star per se. You did but you didn't. He was very insecure. He didn't know where his career was going after he got out of the army."

Love Letters from Elvis

Of course, Elvis had a girl waiting for him back home, Anita Wood, whom he nicknamed "Little."

Never much of a writer, Presley mostly phoned home. But occasionally he put pen to paper.

To a male friend, he wrote complaining about the miserable conditions and being out in the field for fifty days at a time.

To Anita, he wrote that he imagined her lying in his bunk beside him. He claimed he'd desired her so much that he'd break into a sweat just thinking about her. Elvis concluded the letter by asking his "Little" to get a copy of the song "Soldier Boy" and to picture him while listening to it. He signed this very personal letter "Elvis Presley"—in case Anita was confused as to which Elvis might be writing to her!

After they had broken up and Anita was about to marry a professional football player, she thought her husband wouldn't appreciate her hanging on to love letters from another man so she got rid of everything Elvis gave her. In 1991, one of Elvis's letters to Anita resurfaced at a Christie's auction. It sold for $7,700.

Brigitte Bardot Wannabes

Q: Elvis, what would you like to do the most on your first leave in Europe?

EP: I'd like to go to Paris . . . and look up Brigitte Bardot. (1958)

Elvis told a pal that he had been dating a German girl who resembled Bardot. "It's <u>Grind City</u>."

Seventeen-year-old Margit Buergin told a reporter about her famous boyfriend, "He's not at all conceited. He doesn't like to go out often. We spend evenings listening to pop records or he would play the piano and sing folk songs. I was surprised he could play the piano so well. He plays the guitar and says as little as possible about his success as a singer."

Presley was also seeing his secretary Elisabeth Stefaniak, who would jilt him to marry one of his closest army mates, and actress Vera Tschechowa, whom he met during a charity photo shoot.

Miss Bardot herself was represented half-naked in a life-sized poster that hung in his off-base residence. The femme-fatale pose intimidated little Priscilla Beaulieu. "She was the last person I wanted to see, with her fulsome body, pouting lips, and wild mane of tousled hair. Imagining Elvis's taste in women, I felt very young and out of place," she wrote in her autobiography.

Elvis did make it to Paris on leave. Instead of Brigitte Bardot, he dated showgirls.

Q: Where did you spend most of your leave time?
EP: In Paris. I went to Paris. I was in Paris twice.
    Once for ten days and another time for six days.
Q: What do you remember most about those trips?
EP: (whistles) Well, I'll tell you it's a gay town,

I mean, if you like, you know, nightlife, and everything. I went over there to see some of the shows and, you know, to get a touch of the old life. (1960)

Back, and Family-Friendly

Q: What are your plans now that you're leaving the army?

EP: Well, the first thing I plan to do, naturally, is to go home. And then after that I have a television

show with Frank Sinatra some time the later part
of April, then I start work on the picture *GI Blues*
for Paramount, Mr. Wallis, and then after that I
have two pictures with Twentieth Century Fox,
and after that, Heaven knows, I don't know.
(1960)

Like Ed Sullivan before him, Frank Sinatra was on record for
trashing the King of Rock and Roll but was willing to pony up
big money to book the guaranteed ratings getter. Elvis, who
before his army stint was too wild for the Vegas crowd, now
courted that demographic.

Frank and the others surrounded Elvis in his army uniform. Guest Joey Bishop quipped, "Where the heck are his
sideburns?" Elvis responded, "In Germany!"

Singing in a more sophisticated manner, he still moved
enough to get the audience to squeal. But that was no longer a
priority. The new goal was to capitalize on the good will generated by his army stint.

The former rock and roll deviant was now trying to appeal
to everyone from grandmothers to toddlers. His management
decided it was movies, not television or live concerts, where
Presley was going to concentrate his efforts in the future.

March 1958—Arrives for six months of basic training at Fort Hood, Texas.

August 14, 1958—Gladys Presley dies at age forty-six.

September 1958—Shipped off to Germany.

September 1959—Meets future bride, Priscilla Beaulieu.

March 1960—Discharged. Nancy Sinatra welcomes Elvis to the United States as a publicity stunt to promote her father's upcoming television special.

Can't Help Falling in Love

Q: Are you going to keep making films?
EP: I hope to.
Q: What kind?
EP: Well, I'd like to make better films than I made before. (1970)

Hollywood didn't know what to do with Elvis Presley. They put him in movies in which he played un-Elvis characters with names like Walter (twice!!). As if Elvis could ever be named Walter.

Elvis didn't know what to do with Hollywood. Unlike his singing career, where he chose the songs, ran the recording sessions, and put together his own concerts, when it came to movies he was never in the driver's seat.

While today's superstars barely make a movie a year, Presley was cranking out three annually. He rented a mansion in Bel

Air, loaded it up with friends from back home, and returned to Memphis every time a film would wrap. He went to Palm Springs, Hawaii, or Las Vegas for vacation. He recorded sound-track albums and a few nonmovie songs. But mostly, he churned out movies.

'Cause We Are Living in a Material World

Why did Elvis keep doing the movies and the soundtracks? They were extremely lucrative. In 1965, a local Memphis news-paper estimated Elvis earned almost $5.5 million that year. The paper broke it down for his hometown:

$1,000,000	Salary for *Harum Scarum*
650,000	Salary for *Frankie and Johnny*
350,000	Salary for *Paradise, Hawaiian Style*
850,000	Percentage of profits for *Tickle Me*
850,000	Percentage of profits for *Girl Happy*
1,125,000	RCA record royalties
400,000	Music publishing royalties
60,000	Merchandise product royalties

Why Girls Like Elvis Movies

Know why girls love *Change of Habit*? Because it showcases Doctor Elvis. Soldier Elvis more your fantasy? *GI Blues* is the ticket. Dream of a poor Hawaiian beach boy? *Blue Hawaii* has your name all over it. Cowboy Elvis. Indian Elvis. Boat captain Elvis. Photographer Elvis. Blond Elvis. Arab Elvis. Outlaw Elvis. It's like Baskin-Robbins— thirty-one flavors to choose from.

The story may be embarrassing and the songs a waste of his talent, but Elvis wears great clothes and romances up a storm with fabulous costars such as Ann-Margret, Mary Tyler Moore, Ursula Andress, Tuesday Weld, and Nancy Sinatra.

What's not to love?

Even Elvis, who was his harshest critic, admitted in 1972 that his films "worked well on television." Which is where we see them nowadays anyway.

Decoding the Elvis Films

Our special girl guide to Elvis movies is Susan Doll, Ph.D. In addition to penning liner notes for RCA's movie music compilation *Command Performances: The Essential 60's Masters II,* she has written several books on the King including *The Films of Elvis Presley.*

GG2E: You've spent years studying Elvis's film career, can you give us a quick overview of his oeuvre?

SD: When I analyzed his film career, I discovered a couple of things. First, his four films from the 1950s were tailored to suit his image as a notorious rock and roller, his pre-army image designed to attract the teenage audience.

When he returned from the army in 1960, there was a conscious effort to alter his career to reach a wider, more mainstream audience. Part of that plan to alter his image included movies.

Elvis's film image became that of a mainstream leading man: mature, attractive, but not threatening. (Also, any vestige of his Southern background was eliminated from this image.) Thus began a decade of lighthearted musicals that in retrospect have been criticized.

The second thing I discovered was that the bad reputation assigned to these musicals was the result of two things.

One was that Elvis himself was disappointed in them—having never really liked the musical genre to begin with—and he tended to paint them as bad when he was interviewed. Even in concert, he would joke about his "bad" movies.

The second source responsible for denigrating the movies were rock and roll critics and historians, who indirectly "blamed" the movie career for pulling Elvis away from a pure rock and roll singing style. This is a distortion of what happened, but nonetheless that was what these writers, who were the first to write about Elvis in a serious way, propagated.

Don't forget that his lighthearted musicals that everyone makes fun of fit into a genre that was very popular in the early 1960s, which was the teen musical genre. When compared to other musicals of this genre, Presley's were better produced and featured stronger costars (*Viva Las Vegas, Blue Hawaii, Fun in Acapulco*).

One last point, contrary to popular belief, there are a lot of good songs from these films. They are not the pure rockabilly rock and roll preferred by the rock music historians, but they are solid pop tunes that fit the films perfectly.

GG2E: Why would Elvis trash his own movies?

SD: Two reasons, in my opinion. One, Elvis wanted to be a well-respected actor. If you read a lot of original interviews from the 1950s, he talks about it to every reporter. In a couple of interviews, he even claims that he won't sing in films because he is going to be an actor. After his attempt to be an important actor did not work out, at least in the eyes of the Colonel, I think he was profoundly disappointed. As the quality of his movies began to decline (starting with *Kissin' Cousins*), he just gave up. At the end of his film career, he is merely walking through the films with no attempt at "acting."

Two, Elvis never liked musicals personally. He particularly did not like "integrated musicals." An integrated musical is one in which the songs and dances are incorporated into the storyline, which is in opposition to a backstage musical where the singing and dancing take place on a stage or in a show business situation. Integrated musicals are the kind in which the characters break into song and dance at any time.

Viewers tend to either love musicals or hate them. Elvis was in the latter group. He often complained to family and friends that he disliked breaking into song at the drop of a hat on-screen. He felt it made him look ridiculous. Of course, most of his films are integrated musicals. Only a few are backstage musicals.

GG2E: But even Elvis would have to admit that *Blue Hawaii* is a great film! Girls consistently list it as their favorite film.

SD: I think there are several reasons for that. One, it is well crafted. Veteran director Norman Taurog, who was never a great director but a competent one who could do a tightly crafted film, directed it. The costars are good—especially Angela Lansbury. The songs are good and are written by better songwriters than those Elvis would have to contend with later in his film career, when the Colonel began to cut corners.

Two, it became the prototype for the "Elvis musical" that defined the rest of his film career. Thus, it is memorable because it is the turning point in his film career.

Three, the ending, with the Hawaiian wedding, is the epitome of romance in Elvis's films. Many are comic romances, and many end with a wedding. But, often the true romantic flavor of the union between Elvis and the female costar is undercut by comedy or a mediocre song. That is not true here. The Hawaiian wedding is unique looking, it is beautifully photographed, and the song Elvis sings to the girl oozes romance.

GG2E: There's no doubt that Elvis films were popular because they were targeted toward his female fan base. Old newsreels show the hysteria around the opening of *Love Me Tender.* What is it about Elvis films that appeal to girls, other than the appeal of just looking at Elvis?

SD: It's easy to assume his films were targeted toward the female fan base. But, it was more complicated than that, at least at first, and also more shrewd.

When Elvis was discharged from the army, there seemed to be a strategy for reaching a mainstream audience while not losing his core audience of female fans. That means it was a strategy of including everyone and excluding no one.

In 1960, Elvis's choice of music begins to change to a more pop style, a deliberate step away from rock and roll, the music of teenagers. By then Elvis's original teenage fans were older—some married and starting families of their own—so the strategy was that this music would be more acceptable to older listeners, families, men, etcetera, and also appeal to his aging fan base.

Elvis's image became more TV-friendly. He appeared on the Sinatra TV special to introduce his new flavor of music with Sinatra, who, of course, had the widest appeal of any singer at that time. But, Nancy Sinatra was on the special as well, so that the younger fan base didn't feel excluded. See how shrewd the strategy was.

It worked the same way in movies as well. His image evolved from a dangerous or troubled teen into that of a typical leading man. He became a man's man (racecar driver, high diver, boxer, pilot) who could also sing (how romantic for the women).

In the 1950s films, Elvis performed alone on the stage, unless there was a male backup group way in the background. He danced provocatively by gyrating his pelvis which, in the context of the film, drove the girls wild.

In the 1960s, in fast-paced songs, girl dancers most often accompanied Elvis while he sang, and he either danced with them or toned down his gyrations considerably. Scantily clad girls shaking their hips have always been a part of show business, while a male singing star provocatively moving his hips and inciting sexual passion in women has not. hus, his performing style in his movies was mainstreamed, so that it would not be offensive to family audiences.

The thinking was the dancing girls would appease male viewers, while the female audience still had Elvis—a toned-down Elvis, but still Elvis.

Movie Star Threads

"Basically nobody dressed Elvis Presley better than Elvis," wrote the legendary MGM costume designer in her autobiography, *Edith Head's Hollywood.* Head created Elvis's wardrobe for his second film, *Loving You,* and continued to refine his look over the course of his movie career.

She recalled when she first started working with him he was famous for his tight trousers. "So I couldn't change those. Of course, when I look back at the film now, they look like baggy pants. They were tight across the pelvis, but the legs were full." Head added, "His image was very well established, and I wasn't about to tamper with it. In that sense, he was like a male version of Mae West—he knew the Elvis look."

The legendary Head huffed that the Elvis films were no design challenge. In fact, she reduced Elvis's movie wardrobe into a basic uniform. For casual scenes, Elvis would be outfitted in a shirt open at the neck and tight pants ("black jeans were a favorite of his"). When it was time for romance, the uniform would change to dark pants, dark shirt, and a lighter jacket. "There was always a striking contrast between his shirt and his jacket," Ms. Head edified.

Her favorite film to work on? No surprise—*Blue Hawaii*. "Since every film had a theme, I'd have to design something that fit in. In *Blue Hawaii* it was swim trunks with a racing stripe to match his surfboard. The script called for him to get married in traditional Hawaiian groom's garb, so I had a hand in that, too."

Office Romances

Of course, the movies did offer lovely costars for Elvis to romance on- and offscreen.

His *Change of Habit* costar, Mary Tyler Moore, famously quipped that Elvis slept with all of his costars except her, thus forcing every other leading lady to deny affairs. "I resented that," Nancy Sinatra said recently. "She was assuming that I slept with him and I never did. I wish I had . . . but I never did!"

Ann-Margret was the only one who was a serious threat to Elvis's bachelor days. Ironically, previous to their movie together, Ann-Margret starred in *Bye Bye Birdie,* in which she played a typical teenage fan of a singer clearly modeled after Elvis.

At the time of the *Viva Las Vegas* shoot, there were many rumors that she and Elvis were having a fling.

Unfortunately, Ann-Margret remains to this day tight-lipped regarding details. "What we had was very strong and real intense. I knew him very, very well. We were so much alike" is about as indiscreet as she'll get.

She was one of the few Hollywood friends who felt compelled to go to his funeral in Memphis. Her husband accompanied her.

1956—*Love Me Tender* released.

1957—*Loving You*
Jailhouse Rock

1958—*King Creole*

1960—*GI Blues*
Flaming Star

1961—*Wild in the Country*
Blue Hawaii

1962—*Follow That Dream*
Kid Galahad
Girls! Girls! Girls!

1963—*It Happened at the World's Fair*
  Fun in Acapulco

1964—*Kissin' Cousins*
  Viva Las Vegas
  Roustabout

1965—*Girl Happy*
  Tickle Me
  Harum Scarum

1966—*Frankie and Johnny*
  Paradise, Hawaiian Style
  Spinout

1967—*Easy Come, Easy Go*
  Double Trouble
  Clambake

1968—*Stay Away, Joe*
  Speedway
  Live a Little, Love a Little

1969—*Charro!*
  The Trouble With Girls
  Change of Habit

1970—*Elvis: That's The Way It Is*

1973—*Elvis on Tour*

Chapter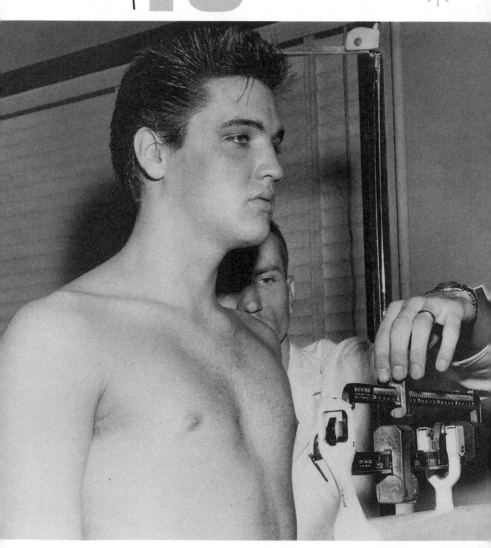

Regarding
Elvis's Weight

Q: Do you watch your food, do you watch your
diet? Do you eat health foods?

EP: I eat health foods and just try to use a little will
power. Don't stuff, you know. In this business
especially in the movies and everything, weight
can be very bad for you. (1962)

Like a female starlet, Elvis was judged by his looks. "It's
very important that for the next picture Elvis look
lean and hard," producer Hal Wallis wrote in a 1961 memo regarding *Blue Hawaii*, a film in which Elvis would appear in a
bathing suit. "He should look very much as he did for *GI Blues*."
Presley's management passed on the request, along with the
suggestion that Elvis might want to purchase an ultraviolet lamp.

THE GIRLS' GUIDE TO ELVIS

But it wasn't just Hollywood producers in the 1960s who were obsessed with Elvis's weight. Thanks to press conference questions in the early years and critical reviewers in the 1970s concert years, Elvis's fluctuating weight has been duly noted and accounted for.

During his early touring days, he would consume an insane amount of food, quickly filling out his skinny teenage six-foot frame. His hyperactivity on stage kept him lean, otherwise "I would get a little round around the tummy, as much as I eat."

As a young man, Elvis could take the pounds off as easily as he put them on. During the Hollywood years, he ate whatever he wanted in the time off between films, then crash dieted before stepping in front of the cameras again.

Once Elvis hit thirty, it got harder to shed the extra pounds. By forty, he would still attempt a starvation diet and managed to temporarily lose a few pounds, but his health was in such bad shape that his body couldn't produce miracles.

In fact, his colon and other health problems worked against him, swelling his midsection to give him a belly he didn't really deserve. Water retention and reaction to medication kept his face puffy. He went on a downslide that could not be reversed and ultimately looked much worse than his actual age.

Desperate Diet Tricks

His personal physi-
cian complained
that Elvis was always
looking for short-
cuts, willing to try
any quick-loss
method he came
across. When
Presley discovered
no-calorie
Jell-O, it was
Jell-O ten times
a day. The "yogurt
diet" was another fad he tried.

More extreme was the "sleep diet" which he attempted in the seventies under the supervision of a Las Vegas doctor. The idea was to give him enough medication to keep him asleep for two weeks, and the weight would just fall off. No wonder Elvis liked this diet! Unfortunately, it didn't work.

To lose weight quickly for the *Aloha* satellite show in 1973, Elvis tried a crazy-sounding yet doctor-recommended plan that involved being injected with the urine of a pregnant woman.

In addition to the injections, he ate no more than five hundred calories a day of dried food. He lost about twenty-five pounds, which he immediately put back on after the television special.

In 1975, he actually tried sensible eating. On the menu: cantaloupe, honeydew melon, apple slices, banana chunks, grapes, and cottage cheese before bed. When he awoke at 5 P.M., he had fruit and an omelet for breakfast. It didn't last long.

Actress Janice Pennington remembered seeing him in Los Angeles, wrapped in Saran Wrap under workout clothes as he tried to sweat the weight off before a Vegas engagement.

Just days before his death, he was back to his last-minute efforts, embarking on a starvation diet to get ready for touring after having several months off. It was the last diet he ever undertook.

Elvis and Food

Q: Getting ready to finish that lunch?
EP: Well, I didn't have enough. They didn't bring
      me but one sandwich and that's just an
      appetizer. (1956)

Elvis's appetite was legendary. An article dating from his days at Sun Records states, "His girlfriend, Dixie, declares that recently at one sitting he ate 8 Deluxe Cheeseburgers, 2 bacon-lettuce-tomato sandwiches—and topped it off with three chocolate milkshakes." When Priscilla first met him in Germany, she sat in the kitchen and watched him devour five "gigantic" bacon sandwiches.

He never lost his taste for the simple, home-cooked foods he grew up with. While other celebrities would be regulars at Hollywood's five-star restaurants, Elvis was happy at home having his full-time cooks fry him up peanut butter and banana sandwiches.

He was also a red meat man. Forget about fish, he hated the smell. "He didn't like chicken much either, and he didn't like turkey," said Graceland cook Mary Jenkins. A vegetable like okra would only make it onto his plate after it had been heavily battered and fried. Even hamburger buns were browned in skillets of melted butter.

When you calculate the calories and fat content of a typical meal prepared in the butter-crazy Graceland kitchen, you can't help but be absolutely horrified.

How to Eat Like Elvis Without Packing on the Pounds

Poor Elvis lived in the era before reduced-fat peanut butter and Wonder bread lite. With the slightest effort (and less King-sized portions), his favorite meals can now be made much more figure-friendly.

Breakfast

Bacon and Biscuits

THE ELVIS WAY:

1 BISCUIT (166 CALORIES, 2 GRAMS FAT);

2 STRIPS PREMIUM BACON (120 CALORIES, 10 GRAMS FAT)

Note: King-size portion is 6 biscuits with a dozen strips of bacon (1,716 calories, 72 grams fat). This is also without Elvis's favorite red-eye gravy, made with the drippings from a pound of bacon and a 1/4 cup of coffee.

THE GIRLS' GUIDE TO ELVIS WAY:

1 BISCUIT (120 CALORIES, 2 GRAMS FAT);

2 STRIPS MEATLESS BACON (45 CALORIES, 1.5 GRAMS FAT)

Bisquick Reduced-Fat Biscuits

2 1/4 cups low-fat Bisquick

3/4 cup skim milk

Preheat oven to 450°. Mix Bisquick with skim milk and when well blended, place on a surface that has been dusted with Bisquick. Roll 10 times. Cut dough into pieces 1/2" thick using a 2 1/2" cookie cutter. Bake on an ungreased cookie sheet for 7–9 minutes or until golden brown. Makes approximately 9 biscuits. Only eat 1 per serving!

Bacon

Cook meatless bacon in the microwave. Remember, bacon
Elvis style is "burnt" (very well done).

*Note: Since 2 strips equal 45 calories and just 1.5 grams of fat, you can
eat a whole package of meatless bacon and not even approach the
calorie and fat content of Elvis's favorite red-eye gravy!*

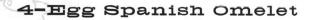

4-Egg Spanish Omelet

THE ELVIS WAY: 1,073 CALORIES, 84.7 GRAMS FAT

THE GIRLS' GUIDE TO ELVIS WAY:
363 CALORIES, 10.7 GRAMS FAT

1 cup Egg Beaters (120 calories, 0 grams fat)

¼ cup reduced-fat cheddar cheese (160 calories, 10 grams fat)

2 tbs. skim milk (20 calories, 0 grams fat)

½ cup chopped bell pepper (12 calories, .2 grams fat)

½ cup chopped onions (27 calories, .2 grams fat)

1 cup diced tomatoes (24 calories, .3 grams fat)

Add milk to the Egg Beaters. Mix in cheese, pepper, onions, and tomatoes. Cook in skillet, coated with Pam or other nonstick spray. Season to taste.

Lunch

Cheeseburger

THE ELVIS WAY: 1,615 CALORIES, 122.5 GRAMS FAT

THE GIRLS' GUIDE TO ELVIS WAY:

255 CALORIES, 8 GRAMS FAT

1 All American–style Boca Burger (110 calories, 3.5 grams fat)

1 slice of reduced-fat American cheese (45 calories, 3 grams fat)

1 slice of onion (9 calories, 0 grams fat)

1 slice of tomato (8 calories, 0 grams fat)

2 pieces of lettuce (3 calories, 0 grams fat)

Wonder bread lite hamburger roll (80 calories, 1.5 grams fat)

Prepare the Boca Burger the fat-free way on the George Foreman mini–kitchen grill (highly, highly recommended). Use the bun-warmer feature on top for a toasty roll.

Note: If you'd prefer a 1/4 pound of extra-lean ground turkey, the count goes down to 205 calories, 6.5 grams fat. Whatever you do, don't eat 8 at a sitting!

Hot Dogs with Sauerkraut

THE ELVIS WAY: 340 CALORIES, 22 GRAMS FAT

THE GIRLS' GUIDE TO ELVIS WAY:

146 CALORIES, 3.5 GRAMS FAT

97% fat-free hot dog (55 calories, 2 grams fat)

Wonder bread lite hot dog roll (80 calories, 1.5 grams fat)

2 tbs. sauerkraut (11 calories, 0 grams fat)

Cook hot dog on grill, or boil in water. Toast roll. Add
sauerkraut. Season to taste.

*Note: This was a true favorite. In later years, when Elvis was hospital-
ized, he'd beg cook Mary Jenkins to smuggle in kraut dogs when she
came to visit. In good health, he'd inhale three at a time.*

Dinner

Pork Chops and Okra

THE ELVIS WAY:

PORK CHOPS (518 CALORIES, 25.3 GRAMS FAT);

FRIED OKRA (707 CALORIES, 60 GRAMS FAT)

THE GIRLS' GUIDE TO ELVIS WAY:

PORK CHOPS (308 CALORIES, 14 GRAMS FAT);

BOILED OKRA (25 CALORIES, 0 GRAMS FAT)

7 oz. center cut pork loin chop (308 calories, 14 grams fat)

½ cup okra (25 calories, 0 grams fat)

Broil or brown the meat in a skillet coated with Pam or other nonstick spray. Prepare and boil fresh okra. Season to taste.

Note: Elvis's mother made okra for him. Her okra was also beloved by Elvis's friend Nick Adams, an actor visiting from Hollywood in 1956. He raved about her cooking during a local radio interview.

Snacks and Dessert

"Fried" Peanut Butter and Banana Sandwiches

THE ELVIS WAY: 745 CALORIES, 53 GRAMS FAT

THE GIRLS' GUIDE TO ELVIS WAY:

375 CALORIES, 13.6 GRAMS FAT

1 medium banana (105 calories, .6 grams fat)

2 slices Wonder bread lite (80 calories, 1 gram fat)

2 tbs. reduced-fat peanut butter (190 calories, 12 grams fat)

Mash the bananas and then mix in peanut butter. (Some people slice bananas on top of the already spread peanut butter, but "mashed and mixed" is the way Graceland cook Mary Jenkins made it.) Lightly toast bread before adding peanut butter and banana spread. Spray frying pan with Pam and brown each side of the sandwich slowly until peanut butter and banana are melted. Or grill in the George Foreman. Just don't smother with butter!

Note: This is perhaps the most famous Elvis snack. "If he wanted them in the 'morning' (when he woke up), I would have to fix them," said cook Mary Jenkins. "If he wanted them at two o'clock in the morning, I would have to still fix them for him. Whenever he'd get a taste for them, he'd call down and that's what he wanted."

Banana Pudding

THE ELVIS WAY: 410 CALORIES, 21 GRAMS FAT

THE GIRLS' GUIDE TO ELVIS WAY:
135 CALORIES, 0 GRAMS FAT

Make from Jell-O banana cream pudding mix and skim milk. To layer the pudding over reduced-fat Nilla Wafer cookies and sliced bananas (in true Elvis style), add 120 calories, 2 grams fat for one serving of cookies and 105 calories, .6 grams fat for one medium banana.

Note: Of course, Graceland cooks made the pudding from scratch, but who has time for that!

Pound Cake with Peaches and Cream

THE ELVIS WAY: 1,102 CALORIES, 64 GRAMS FAT

(BASED ON A ¼ POUND CAKE SERVING)

THE GIRLS' GUIDE TO ELVIS WAY:

370 CALORIES, 11 GRAMS FAT

Sara Lee reduced-fat pound cake (280 calories, 11 grams fat)

1 cup canned peaches, packed in water (58 calories, 0 grams fat)

4 tbs. fat-free cream (32 calories, 0 grams fat)

Slice pound cake into reasonably sized servings. Top with sliced canned peaches and cream. Substitute fresh peaches whenever possible. Elvis preferred half-and-half, but whipped cream is always an option.

Note: This is a quick and easy dessert from Elvis's California days. Even the most dedicated bachelor can make it!

1953—Writes 150 pounds on an employment record (age eighteen).

1958—Weighs 180 pounds going into the army.

1967—Noticeable roll of fat in *Paradise, Hawaiian Style.*

1968—Thinner than ever for the television special. Claims he lost ten pounds while doing the show.

1971—Starting to put on weight.

1973—Crash diets in January for the *Aloha* satellite special.

1973—In May, *Variety* reports "Elvis is neither looking or sounding good. Some thirty pounds overweight, he is puffy, white faced and blinking against the light."

1973—Tries the "sleep diet."

1975—Fat and forty.

1976—A diet of yogurt, lots of vegetables, and low-cholesterol bacon strips.

1977—Allows himself to be filmed for a CBS concert special despite being very overweight.

Chapter 11

Perfect Hair

"I stopped using that greasy kid stuff just like everybody else did."
ELVIS AT THE MADISON SQUARE GARDEN
PRESS CONFERENCE (1972)

Before filming began on *Roustabout*, producer Hal Wallis wrote a memo to Presley's management complaining that Elvis's hair looked like a wig in his previous film, *Viva Las Vegas*, which Wallis did not produce. This "could have a very detrimental effect on his entire career," Wallis warned.

With official studio memos flying back and forth, you'd think Elvis was the second coming of Samson. Who knew his hair was the source of his power?

Although he certainly spent a lot of time on it, Elvis didn't seem to mind when the result of his careful combing went astray. He let it flop every which way it wanted to whenever he sang, both in the 1950s and 1970s. Girls itched to run their fingers through those free-flowing locks—and often got a chance as he leaned down for a kiss.

It is true that sometimes during the Hollywood movie years Elvis's hair seemed artificially frozen and forbidding. There was even a period when he experimented with no sideburns— and worse, bangs! It was not pretty.

Then in the 1970s the hair got bigger, longer, more teased— and the sideburns got huge. But hey, it was the seventies and there was a lot of bad hair going around.

P.S. We all know those ink-black locks were not God-given. His natural hair color was light brown. Before he began dyeing it, the pomade he used made it look darker.

Only His Hairdresser Knows for Sure

Larry Geller was styling hair at Jay Sebring's salon, the epicenter of young, happening Hollywood, when he got a call to do Elvis's hair. Larry immediately became a confidant and loyal lifelong friend. On August 17, 1977, he went to the Memphis funeral home to do the King of Rock and Roll's hair for the last time.

GG2E: We know you were much more than a hairdresser
to Elvis. As you revealed in your own book *If I
Can Dream,* your shared spiritual interests were

the most important part of the relationship.
But we girls like to get to the root of things:
roots, follicles, and pores. Tell us about your
first time cutting Elvis's hair.

LG: One afternoon in 1964, I was styling Johnny
Rivers's hair at the salon, when my phone rang.
It was one of Elvis's aides, asking if I'd come up
to Elvis's home. At that point, working with
Hollywood celebrities, everyone from Frank
Sinatra to Peter Sellers to Steve McQueen, was
almost second nature to me. But the thought of
meeting Elvis—it was exciting. It really was.

So I drove up to Elvis's home in Bel Air.
When I got to his street, I knew exactly what
house it was because there were dozens of people
outside the gates. Mostly women, but a lot of
guys. Elderly people, young people. People
taking pictures. As I drove through the gates,
they were screaming, "Tell Elvis I love him. Tell
him I'm here."

Well, I walked into Elvis's home on Perugia
Way. I looked to my right and saw Elvis sitting
at a table with a few guys. He motioned to me,
"Hey, man, I'll be right with you in a minute."
Someone ushered me into his den, and about a
minute later, Elvis introduced himself.

When we went into his bathroom, I assumed I would see a luxurious beauty salon—type chair that reclined. It was nothing like that. It was just a bathroom. I mean, it was a nice-sized bathroom, but none of the trimming that I expected.

He dunked his head right into the basin.

GG2E: Just like a normal sink?

LG: Just like a normal sink. Like a normal guy. He explained to me that he's in the middle of a film called *Roustabout* with Barbara Stanwyck so his hair should kind of match the way it is right now. Because I'm looking in the mirror, I could see his eyes following every move I made.

GG2E: Talk about pressure! Did you have any trouble?

LG: He had a full head of beautiful hair, but it was very, very weak. Baby fine. So I blew it dry. As I'm blowdrying it, I realized it needed some body. I spritzed it with hairspray. Put a little extra amount on it, blew it dry.

It looked just the way I wanted it to look. As I'm kind of molding the hair, I say, "Well, what do you think, Elvis?" He looks and he says, "Oh, great, great." He saw right away it was the way it should be.

That was the beginning.

GG2E: At the salon, you were working with the hottest Hollywood stars. How did Elvis stack up?

LG: I've been around Paul Newman and others who had great faces of our time. No one looked like Elvis. And from every angle he would look different. He had what we call a "trick face." Some people just look the same: monochromatic. He was multidimensional.

He had the most beautiful hair, the most beautiful face. Even at the very end of his life, when he was very, very ill. When we were on tour, he would wake up very late in the afternoon, and I would walk in when he had just opened his eyes. Here's a guy who has glaucoma, hypertension, a spastic colon, his blood sugar is off the chart, his cholesterol—this man was so sick, but he looked so beautiful.

GG2E: You said he had baby-fine hair. What products did you use to combat this?

LG: Elvis had beautiful hair, but because it was so weak, I knew to stay away from shampoos that you buy in beauty salons or in the market.

The only shampoo I would use is something from the health store—as a base! It would have to be pH balanced. A very mild shampoo without all the detergents. No alkalinity.

I heard about this doctor from Mexico who had this new deal called jojoba. No one had even heard about it—I'm talking about back in '75 or '74. At that time a little tiny bottle was $20—and that was $20 then!

I put that in, plus pure 99 percent alovera. Some biotin. I would puncture vitamin E caps and squeeze them in. And I would shake up the whole thing. I probably looked like an alchemist, you know, in Elvis's bathroom doing this. "Hey, man, whatever you're doing, just keep on doing it," he'd say. "Just make sure of one thing, make sure I keep my hair."

I used special stuff on Elvis. Not only that, I would massage Elvis's scalp as often as I could. I would give it a very nice brushing after the shampoo to lubricate the hair shaft and protect it. Because remember, I'm dyeing his hair. So I'm trying to offset and counterbalance all the harm that dyes and peroxide did to the hair.

GG2E: What about the dye, was that homemade too?

LG: No, no, that was not. I used different brands over the years. You know, Clairol, L'Oréal.

GG2E: You did his hair both for the movies and for his personal life. Was there any difference?

LG: In the movies, it was very similar. Elvis always wanted his hair sprayed. In the seventies, it became longer, and he added the sideburns. It still needed to be done, but it wasn't as set, as molded, as perfect like it looked in the sixties. When he was on the stage, he was moving, and his hair would sort of, you know, it looked great, then it started getting messed up. But it didn't matter, because that looked great. It was natural.

GG2E: So when he was making the movies, what did he look like "in real life"—his time at home. Did he have an "off-duty" hairstyle?

LG: Well, every night Elvis would have the girls come over to the house. They were all outside anyway. At a certain time, a certain amount would be allowed to come in. The guys would say, "You, you, you and you." Before this Elvis and I would be in the bathroom for an hour or two, doing his hair. He'd have his hair done every night.

GG2E: Every night?

LG: Every night. Yeah.

GG2E: That's why he needed you full time! What about shaving, did he do it himself?

LG: He absolutely did.

GG2E: An electronic shaver or regular razor?

LG: Both. And he would shave several times a day.

GG2E: So he always looked pretty much the same.

LG: Always the same, yeah.

GG2E: Why do you think Elvis's hair is so iconic?

LG: Because it was perfect hair. Perfect for his face and his persona.

GG2E: You did his hair for the funeral. What was that like?

LG: His father said, "Larry, you've got to go and fix Elvis's hair. You got to make him look the way you know he's supposed to look." So the next morning at eight, I went to the mortuary with Charlie Hodge.

GG2E: Had you ever done a corpse before?

LG: Never. And I never will again.

I looked down at his hair, and I realized, "Oh no, I was supposed to dye his hair." I didn't bring anything, I wasn't thinking straight. He had half an inch of regrowth of gray hair— all over!

I'm thinking, "Oh, my God, what am I going to do?" You know you have to get very creative at certain times. Well, there were several morticians working on Elvis's hands. One was a woman. I said, "Do you have your mascara?" She gave me the little mascara kit with a teeny-weeny brush. It was black. I spit in it, schmeered it on—and it worked.

I can't even begin to tell you how long it took me to do his hair. His hair wouldn't cooperate. So you know what I did? I ratted it. Yeah, I ratted his hair. Then I brushed it very, very softly and spritzed it. It looked perfecto.

One other thing. Everyone's heard stories about Elvis faking his death. Absurd, ludicrous, absurd, nonsense, no way. First of all, there is no way you can simulate a head of hair. In fact, even with hair transplants, you can't simulate a head of hair. After doing Elvis's hair not once, not a hundred, but thousands and thousands of times during his life, I can say that was his hair.

April 30, 1964—Larry Geller begins cutting Elvis's hair.

August 17, 1977—Elvis's hair styled for the last time.

Chapter 12

Being Mrs. Presley

Q: If you found someone while you were in the army that you felt you were in love with, would you get married in service?

EP: Uh, I don't think so, sir. Because the way I look at it, if you find someone that you're in love with, and she's in love with you, she will understand about my career and she will— She won't want to do anything to hurt it. So she wouldn't rush me, in other words. (1958)

Priscilla certainly didn't rush him.

They met in Germany in 1959 when she was fourteen. He was twenty-four. But remember, Jerry Lee Lewis had recently wed a thirteen-year-old, and Loretta Lynn also married at age thirteen. So Elvis wasn't alone in romancing the underaged.

When Elvis left Germany, he gave Priscilla one of his army jackets. Sharon Purkey Fields, classmate at Priscilla's high school in Germany, reported that Priscilla proudly hung the field jacket over her bedroom desk.

Elvis imported Priscilla twice for short visits before wrangling a permanent arrangement when she was a senior in high school. The official line was she was a family friend staying with Vernon Presley and his new wife while attending Catholic school to finish her education.

His Not So Secret Girlfriend

"Everyone knew from the day he met her in Germany that she was somebody important in his life," said gossip hound Rona Barrett. "All those stories about how he asked her parents if she could come and live in Graceland. All of this was known and never really kept a secret. When he said to you, 'I treat her like a sister or a family member or somebody like that,' you knew Elvis was telling the truth because there were never any stories of Elvis being abusive or taking advantage of women."

Sandra Harmon, coauthor of Priscilla's autobiography, said, "By the time they got married, it was about doing the right thing, since the girl had been whisked away from her house when she was sixteen and was known to be living with him. There was nowhere to go but marriage. Elvis couldn't kick her out. His image would have been horrible if he had done that."

According to Priscilla, he proposed to her on Christmas Eve 1966 in her bathroom while she was brushing her hair.

"Everybody was trying to figure out when and where they would ever get married," said Rona Barrett, who scooped everyone by being the first to report that the wedding was taking place. "There had been so many reports over the years they had been together that this was the year they were getting married, this was the week they were getting married, this was the month they were getting married. None of which ever proved to be true."

On May 1, 1967, it proved to be true. The private ceremony was held at Las Vegas's Aladdin Hotel in the early morning. A press conference and breakfast reception followed. The newlyweds then flew back to Palm Springs to honeymoon.

The Ultimate Elvis Wedding in Vegas— Then and Now

Then

Officiator: Nevada Supreme Court Justice David Zenoff.

Time: 9:41 A.M.

Place: Private suite of the Aladdin Hotel owner.

Best men: Elvis's staff members Joe Esposito and Marty Lacker.

Maid of honor: Priscilla's sister, Michelle Beaulieu.

Groom's tuxedo: Black brocade silk.

Bridal gown: White silk chiffon.

Press coverage: The local Memphis paper's headline reported, "Wedding Is Typically Elvis— Quick, Quiet and In Style."

Exploitation: Newsreel coverage of the event and press conference. Photo of groom Elvis and bride Priscilla later inserted as a bonus into *Clambake* soundtrack albums.

Now

Officiator: A jumpsuited Elvis impersonator.

Place: The Elvis Chapel in Las Vegas.

Exploitation: The "Elvis Special" includes twenty-four photos and a videotape of the ceremony.

Married to Elvis

"Sometimes I think if I knew then what I know now—that only when you're a person in your own right can you help another person be happy—I could have made our marriage work. But there was no way I could have become my own person in that marriage," Priscilla explained long after she ceased being Mrs. Presley.

"Priscilla was very meek and really didn't do or say much of anything," reported one of the girls who hung around outside the gates of the Presley Hollywood home. "She took French lessons, she took ballet lessons. She had her hair done, she had her nails done. Later on she took karate lessons. And in between she did a lot of shopping."

In other words, she was officially a Beverly Hills housewife—at age twenty-one. And by twenty-two, she was a mother, giving birth to the King's only heir, Lisa Marie Presley.

Life After Elvis, but Still Mrs. Presley

"Raised" by Elvis to be a trophy wife, she was determined to stand tall—all five-foot-four of her—from the moment she broke out of Graceland. When she first left him to find happiness, personal growth, and hot sex with a karate champion, she opened a boutique with a friend. Which makes sense considering Priscilla's training was primarily in shopping. Later she became a commercial spokeswoman, doing ads for shampoos, cars, diet drinks, and hair-extension products. Over the decades she added actress, best-selling author, producer, motion picture studio board member, and perfume maven to her résumé.

But where she's really made her mark is running the Elvis business better than her ex-husband ever did.

Working Woman magazine praised her in 1993, stating, "Certainly she has done what he was never able to do: organize his business affairs, hire savvy advisers and create and manage a thriving enterprise based on his work and image. If Elvis helped to create Priscilla as a young woman, she, in turn, has helped to make him what he is today."

She is currently the chairman of the advisory board for his estate.

September 1959—At age fourteen, Priscilla meets Elvis.

March 1960—Elvis makes a "It was no big romance" statement about Priscilla at a press conference after returning home from the army.

March 1963—Priscilla moves to Memphis permanently to finish high school.

May 1, 1967—Becomes Mrs. Elvis Presley.

February 1, 1968—Gives birth to Lisa Marie nine months to the day from their wedding night.

December 1971—Leaves Elvis for married-with-children karate champion Mike Stone.

August 1977—Presides over Elvis's funeral.

June 26, 1979—Vernon Presley dies, leaving Priscilla coexecutor of Elvis's estate, as trustee for Lisa Marie.

September 2000—Elected to the board of Metro-Goldwyn-Mayer, the studio for which Elvis made the bulk of his movies. Other board members include Kirk Kerkorian, Francis Ford Coppola, and General Alexander Haig.

Chapter

Sex with Elvis

EP: You know that girl I was with last night?
Friend: That dog?
EP: Oh, man, she gave great head, boy. Hey, Joe,
that chick last night gave the greatest head.
(1972)

Elvis would be appalled by how much we know about his sex life. Thanks to tell-alls from his ex-wife, girl-friends, and staff, everything from his uncircumcised penis to his underwear fetish is now public record. In truth, his sexual quirks were not that kinky—just strange and uniquely Elvis.

His poor girlfriends were forever puzzled by his inclinations. Too often they questioned their own sexuality rather than his.

If only there had been a *Girls' Guide to Elvis* back then, giving them "dos and don'ts" regarding sex with Elvis.

DO: Give Great Head (see quote above)

DON'T: Expect King-sized

One biographer reported that a female bedmate described the six-foot-tall Elvis as "on the slight side of normal."

"He was not hung very well. He was just average-sized, maybe even a little smaller than average," an anonymous source revealed to another biographer.

DO: Be Prepared for an Early Exit

An army buddy said Elvis told him that pulling out and finishing the job himself was his preferred way of preventing pregnancy.

"I remember the first time we had sex and he masturbated instead of having completed intercourse," said seventies-era girlfriend Sheila Ryan. "I was devastated. I thought, 'Oh my God, I'm not enough. What's the matter with me?'"

DO: Wear Plain White Undies

DON'T: Bikini Wax

Barbara Leigh, who dated him in 1970, reported, "He liked certain things, like white lace panties with a bit of pubic hair coming out the sides. He told me that was very important because when he was a young boy of 13 or 14, he tumbled around with some girls in the yard and saw their white panties."

DO: Bring a Friend and Plenty of Film

"He was a classic voyeur," according to Sandra Harmon, who cowrote Priscilla's autobiography. "He took hundreds of stills of Priscilla alone and films of her prancing around with other girlfriends."

The best man at Elvis's wedding talked about Priscilla wrestling with girls at Elvis's request in his tell-all book: "He was particularly turned on by two girls together, a relatively innocent fantasy. Elvis convinced Priscilla to perform while he played video director. Though he appears in a couple of shots, Elvis is always in his pajamas, never naked, as has been reported. I've seen many of the tapes, and they wouldn't even merit an 'R' rating in today's mainstream movies."

DON'T: Have a Baby

In a tell-all published while Elvis was still alive, one of his oldest friends revealed the King's biggest phobia: "He had a thing about if a woman he was screwing had a baby. Something in him just turned off when he learned a woman had had a baby. It's quite a strange hang-up."

Priscilla found out right after Lisa Marie's birth that this quirk applied to her, too. Girlfriend Joyce Bova, who called him "a gentle, considerate lover," reported in her autobiography that she had an abortion after realizing how adamant Elvis was. "I found it to be very odd," remarked live-in lover Linda Thompson. "It didn't make me anxious to have his child."

"We all have our preferences, likes and dislikes," Priscilla dismissed the fuss about her ex-husband's sex life decades after his death. "Elvis was no different. And the things that he liked and enjoyed were harmless."

1948/9—Pubescent wrestling with girls begins white-underwear fetish that will haunt him his entire life.

1967—Marries Priscilla, impregnates her on their wedding night.

1968—Will no longer have sex with Priscilla after she gives birth.

1972—Makes indiscreet "great head" comment while the *Elvis on Tour* camera crew is filming. The clip isn't used in that documentary but surfaces in the theatrical version of the posthumous *This Is Elvis* (dubbed with the euphemistic "could raise the dead" in the TV and home-video version).

Chapter **14**

MEMORIESTHE'68COMEBACKSPECIAL

The Comeback

Q: For many years you were only available to the
   public in films. Why return to performing?
EP: I think the most important thing is the
   inspiration I got from a live audience, I was
   missing that. (1970)

Except for a few one-off benefit concerts in the early
1960s, from the time he went into the army until
1968, the King of Rock and Roll was not allowed to play for
his loyal subjects.

In '68, Elvis returned to performing before screaming
girls in his very own television special. Originally titled *Singer
Presents Elvis* (Singer Sewing Machines was the sponsor), it's now
known as the *'68 Comeback Special.*

"He was worried that nobody was going to come to the
tapings," said Sandi Miller, a fan whom Elvis personally invited
to be part of the studio audience. "Every day he would ask,

'You're going to come, aren't you?' After it was all over with, the next time I saw him, I got twenty questions: 'What did you think? What was your favorite part? What part didn't you like? Was it loud enough?' He wanted input left and right. He was insecure about it."

The special was a smash. Afterward, the network proudly took out ads proclaiming "More women age 18 to 49 watched his TV special than any other in '68."

Black Leather

Not being terribly familiar with Elvis's history, *'68 Special* costume designer, Bill Belew, mistakenly assumed Presley had worn leather during the early rock and roll years. "He may have worn a leather jacket, but that's about it. At that time, though, we were into denim, and I said, 'What if I just duplicate a denim outfit in black leather?' Elvis loved it."

The trademark high "Napoleonic" collar (ending just below the ear) also debuted with the leather suit. Belew liked it because it framed Presley's face.

Although it was a new look for Elvis, Belew knew immediately that it was right for him.

Elvis hired Belew to design all future stage costumes and personal wardrobe. Thus began a partnership that would result in another signature look: the jumpsuits.

Live in Concert, Elvis-style

Q: Is your stage presentation still the same way it was, or have you improved on that?

EP: I just do whatever I feel, onstage. You know, I've always done that. (1970)

After the *'68 Special,* Elvis assembled a band, put together a set list, and returned to live performing. It was his show, and he was the show. No dancing girls surrounding him. No elaborate sets, lighting, or production numbers. Just a man in a jumpsuit surrounded by James Burton on lead guitar, John Wilkinson on rhythm guitar, Charlie Hodge on guitar and vocals (and water and scarf duty), Jerry Scheff on the fender bass, Glen Hardin on piano, Ronnie Tutt on drums, vocalist Kathy Westmoreland, The Sweet Inspirations, and a male quartet (the Imperials or the Stamps). And, of course, Joe Guercio leading the orchestra. Yep, an orchestra.

Sometimes the back-up musicians or singers would be different. Sometimes the songs would be different. Sometimes Elvis wore a two-piece outfit instead of a jumpsuit. Sometimes he performed for thirty minutes. Sometimes he performed for two hours. But no matter the variations, it was always Elvis that the people came to see.

How did these concerts differ from those of the 1950s?

With technically superior sound systems and less teenage shrieking in the audience, the audience could now hear Elvis. "When Elvis was in true form, he was fabulous," said Sweet Inspiration Myrna Smith. "His voice was a lot more remarkable than it ever came off on record."

"His music repertoire was unbelievable," pointed out RCA executive Joan Deary. "Who else do you know in rock 'n' roll that could sing 'The American Trilogy' or 'How Great Thou Art,' and would do it live on stage?"

Just as he had done in the 1950s, Elvis covered other people's hits as part of his stage show: The Beatles ("Something," "Get Back" which he spliced together with his own "Little Sister"), Three Dog Night ("Never Been to Spain"), Neil Diamond ("Sweet Caroline"), James Taylor ("Steamroller Blues"), Simon and Garfunkel ("Bridge Over Troubled Water"), Creedence Clearwater Revival ("Proud Mary"), and even Olivia Newton-John ("Let Me Be There," "If You Love Me [Let Me Know]").

RCA executive Joan Deary summed up the Elvis concert experience, "When people went to see him, they didn't care what he said; what mattered was the feeling he put into a song. They knew he put everything he had into every song he sang. He and the audience had a love affair."

Jumpsuits!

For his return to performing, Elvis turned to the man who made the wonderful 1968 television-special clothes, Bill Belew. Inspired by Elvis's lifelong interest in karate, Belew improvised a new look based on the martial arts garb. The collars were high to frame his face, the neckline dipped low to show off his chest, and eye-catching belts brought attention to his famous pelvis.

The two-piece suits quickly became one-piece to better withstand the wear and tear of Elvis's movements. And thus the jumpsuits were born. Belew imported 100-percent-wool gabardine fabric from Milan, the same material ice-skaters used for their costumes.

The simple designs became elaborate. All were Belew's ideas, which Elvis approved. Suits weighed anything from twenty-five pounds to three times that. Although Elvis was always game to try something new, if the fans didn't react well to an outfit or a color, he stopped wearing it.

Then there were the capes. When Elvis added them (they were attached with hooks, eyes, and velcro), the look was set. *Chicago Tribune* reporter Linda Winer nailed it on the head when she said in 1972 that Elvis looked like "a white Batman dressed formal." Elvis admitted that when he read comic books as a child he pictured himself as the hero. His dream was now a reality.

Isn't He a Doll?

The makers of the Barbie doll are issuing a series of Elvis dolls. To symbolize the jumpsuit years, the doll wears the famous American-eagle suit worn on the *Aloha* satellite special. The real suit cost approximately $65,000 in 1973 dollars. The doll's outfit isn't quite that elaborate, but it does come complete with its own scarf to throw. What's underneath the suit? Let's just say the doll follows the established Ken doll modus operandi.

Jumpsuit Secrets

Wash with Woolite? The jumpsuits were sent to the dry cleaners just like Elvis's normal clothes.

Sized to fit? When the suits got too tight around the waist and couldn't be let out anymore, Elvis had to get smaller. Manned with giant rolls of Saran Wrap, his staff would tightly bind his midsection. An instant fix, albeit one that made it hard to breathe.

Feel a breeze back there? The jumpsuits didn't solve the "splitting the pants" problem that had plagued Elvis from day one. Elvis told the *Elvis on Tour* documentary crew that during his first Vegas appearance he ripped so many suits—almost a dozen—that "the audience thought it was a part of the show!"

V.P.L.? What Elvis wore under the body-clinging suits also came from designer Bill Belew. They were described as "elastic undershorts." They didn't leave a line.

Scarf Wars

"Don't be so rough on the people when they come back here. They just come to get scarves. Don't treat them like they're going to jail, goddamnit," Elvis scolded bouncers at a concert in the 1970s.

You know how some guys go to baseball games with their mitts, hoping to catch a fly ball? Well, at an Elvis concert it was the girls who were intent on catching a flying scarf.

When he first returned to performing, Elvis relied on women to provide cloths to dry his face. In the *'68 Special,* girls sitting ringside had to dig into their purses to find tissues.

Soon, rather than taking cloths from fans, he was giving them his. At first, it was the scarf he wore for the full concert. Then it became scarves by the trunkload. Literally, he'd order them in bulk. The women scrambled like wild things trying to get these precious, sweat-anointed souvenirs. "There were people who would try to pull them out of your hand," said frequent concertgoer Robin Rosaaen, who collected thirteen in total.

Having Fun with Elvis Onstage

No air kisses for Elvis. He always locked lips when he greeted female fans during "Love Me Tender."

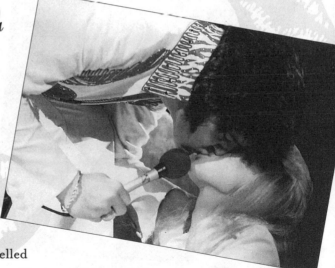

To those who yelled out their love to him, Elvis would tease with statements like "Honey, I love you too, but what can I do about it onstage? Maybe we can arrange something after the show." This is the same man who would say at the Madison Square Garden press conference that he had to go back to rehearsal—unless the female reporter had something better in mind.

Words weren't all Elvis had to offer. Sometimes there was a noticeable "rise" happening below the belt. "You couldn't take your eyes off of it," reported one fan. Photos were eagerly snapped and traded among his female followers.

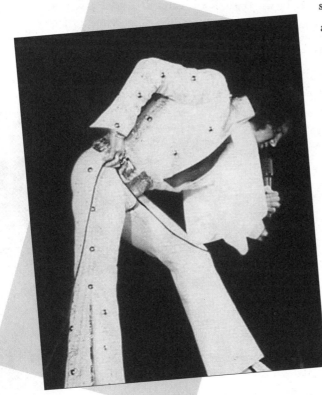

In the book *Did Elvis Sing in Your Hometown, Too?* which reports on every single Elvis concert in the 1970s, author Lee Cotton tallies up a typical Elvis concert—Cleveland Coliseum, 1975. "Elvis was on stage

approximately an hour, performed 21 songs, handed out 36
scarves, and kissed 20 ladies."

"Husbands still scoffed. Wives still screamed," summed up
Linda Winer in a 1972 *Chicago Tribune* review. "He kissed a few
never-to-be-forgotten kisses, tossed a few perspiration-soaked
scarves, graciously accepted the proffered lingerie. Crouched
and karate-chopping, he teased the audience into perfectly
controlled, orderly, well behaved hysteria."

December 3, 1968—The *'68 Special* airs on NBC at 9 P.M.

September 1970—Tours for the first time since 1957.

June 26, 1977—Last concert performance, Market Square Arena in Indianapolis.

Chapter 15

La Vida Loca

*"They're gonna put me away, man, I know it. It's
just a matter of time, boy."*

ELVIS, ONSTAGE (1970)

fter getting out of the army in 1960, Elvis's life was already heavily scheduled for the next decade. But once
he got out from under the movie contracts and began a routine
of Vegas appearances and U.S. concert tours in the 1970s, he
had much more time on his hands.

Elvis with time on his hands was not a good thing. Crazy
things happened. And Elvis's life from 1970 to 1977 was full of
crazy things.

Elvis Drops by the White House

*"I would love to meet you just to say hello if you're not too busy.
Respectfully, Elvis Presley."*

ELVIS'S LETTER TO PRESIDENT NIXON (1970)

It's such an odd story that there was even a TV movie made about it. Elvis loved to collect things, especially police badges. Around Christmastime 1970, he became obsessed with getting a federal narcotics bureau badge. In one of the few times he ever traveled by himself, he flew to Washington, D.C., on the spur of the moment to see about wrangling himself the badge. When it turned out to be a little harder than expected, he wrote a letter to Nixon and showed up at the White House to convince the president to give him the badge.

Elvis's unique "come a'visitin'" ensemble threw Nixon aide Bud Krogh, who took note of everything from the "tight-fitting dark velvet pants" to the "dark purple velvet cape." Dressed in the color of kings, Elvis also wore more gold than Midas: a medallion around his neck and "around his waist was a belt with a huge four-inch by six-inch gold belt buckle with a complex design I couldn't make out without embarrassing myself."

If Krogh had asked, Elvis would have been glad to show off the belt—as he would later do at the Madison Square Garden press conference. It was the "championship" belt, reportedly valued at $10,000, he was awarded by the International Hotel a few months earlier for the record-setting attendance at his shows. Elvis figured it went well with everything and wore it with jumpsuits and everyday outfits. After all, if you're wearing a cape, your accessories really have to be big and noticeable to compete.

When a Cadillac Just Won't Do: What to Give a President

Elvis the gun collector thought the president might like an antique gun. When the Secret Service wouldn't let him take it into the Oval Office, Elvis produced more personal mementos: 8" × 10" glossy photos of his family, including his baby daughter.

Lucy:

Elvis Presley (believe it or not) was granted an appointment with the President on Monday, Dec. 21. He left these autographed photos with the President. I don't think any acknowledgment would be necessary. For your good disposition!

Bev.

Recd. gun previously –

Nixon responded with a gift of the coveted badge. Mission accomplished.

Girls on the Side

Just because he married Priscilla didn't mean Elvis was going to settle down and be a one-woman man. Having girlfriends was even easier when he was on tour. He could import and export in bulk numbers.

With his concerts becoming rote, a constant influx of girls provided some variety to his life.

At first, he explained to each new girl that he and Priscilla had an open marriage. Most of the girls were "nice girls" concerned about dating a married man. Only when Priscilla left him could he use the magic word "separated." Then finally "divorced."

In direct contrast to Priscilla, who preferred to stay in Los Angeles, the new girls were expected to go with him as he toured.

Perhaps the ultimate tourist was Linda Thompson, who was with Elvis from 1972 to 1976.

Ten years after Elvis's death, Linda explained why they never married.

Although she had been interested in making their relationship legal, "By the time he was ready, I realized that wasn't the way I wanted to live for the rest of my life."

Cadillacs for Everyone!

One way Elvis generated excitement was by going on frequent shopaholic binges.

Biographer Jerry Hopkins pointed out, "It's unusual that a man's jeweler becomes a significant source of information in writing a biography."

Elvis's jewelers saw quite a lot of him in the later years as his own body became heavily bejeweled and customized jewelry was handed out like party favors.

Elvis even invented his own jewelry: TCB pendants for his male coterie and TLC for the women. "Elvis knew exactly what he wanted," said one of his jewelers, Lowell Hays. "Elvis bought very nice pieces of jewelry. He was not cheap."

The jewelry blowouts were nothing compared to the car extravaganzas. On one out-of-control spree in 1975, he spent $140,000 on thirteen Cadillacs earmarked for family and friends and one for a woman who just happened to be window shopping at the dealership when Elvis arrived. "You don't expect to find him on a car lot at that time of night," said the lucky Mennie L. Person. "Put it on the list," Elvis told the car salesman when Ms. Person chose an $11,500 El Dorado.

Elvis Presley Airlines

In 1975, Elvis bought his own plane. Not content to merely refurbish the Convair 880 jet previously used by Delta Airlines, Elvis was determined to customize it like he did his Cadillacs. Gold everywhere. Of course, a big old TCB logo had to be painted on the tail (to match the one painted on the wall in Graceland's TV room). His daughter's name was inscribed on the bow.

Elvis was so excited about his new purchase that he would often take friends down to Dallas just to inspect the ongoing alterations.

Once the plane was fully operational, Elvis thought nothing of climbing aboard and jetting to Denver for mondo peanut butter, jelly, and bacon sandwiches made by the Colorado Gold Mine Company. His staff called ahead and had twenty-two of the "Fools Gold" specials delivered to the airport, where he dined on the *Lisa Marie* with his staff and friends from the Denver police force, before flying back to Memphis. That's living!

Something from ELVIS' wardrobe for you.

RCA Records

Wardrobe Genocide

RCA came up with a unique promotional idea for another greatest hits collection: cut up the King's wardrobe and include a swatch in each boxed set. Elvis, who was increasingly phobic about recording new material, eagerly shipped cases and cases to RCA. Among the many garments needlessly slaughtered were the *'68 Special*'s faux gold lamé jacket and the Nudie-designed *Clambake* suit.

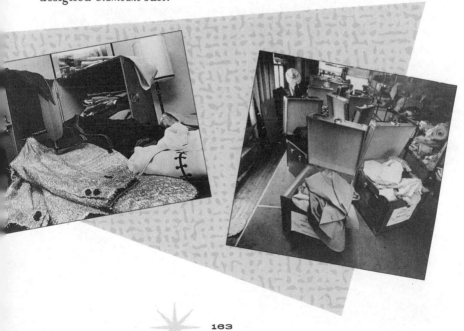

September 1970—Awarded a championship belt from the International Hotel for setting attendance records.

December 1970—Visits with Tricky Dick.

August 1971—*Elvis: The Other Sides—Worldwide Gold Award Hits, Vol. 2* issued with desperate "piece of Elvis's wardrobe for you" ploy.

October 1973—Overweight, wears a sweatsuit to his divorce hearing.

April 1975—How many other little girls have a plane named after them?

July 27, 1975—Makes a car salesman working on commission very happy.

February 1976—Day trip to Denver for sandwiches.

Fat and Forty

EP: When we're not performing, we're on route to
somewhere else.

Q: Doesn't it get you down?

EP: Well, it does, but I haven't been in it long
enough yet for it really to show up on me.
(1956)

A h, youth. By the time he hit the big 4-0, it was showing
up on him and almost every concert reviewer felt the
need to point this out.

A report of his 1975 New Year's Eve concert blamed "middle-
age spread" for Elvis's splitting his pants during the concert,
willfully ignoring that busting out the seat of his trousers had
been a problem since the 1950s.

One reviewer in 1976 flat-out stated, "Not only is he fat,
his stomach hangs over his belt, his jowls hang over his collar
and his hair hangs over his eyes." Yet another, "Elvis is fat, and

there's no hiding it. His cheeks are puffy and he has a double chin."

Desperate Times Require Desperate Measures

In June 1975, Elvis got a minifacelift and eye job. His regular doctors tried to talk him out of it, saying it was completely unnecessary. But like a vain actress who believes it's never too early to begin the facelift years, Elvis was taking all the criticism about his aging too much to heart. Did the plastic surgery improve his looks? Several of his staff members reported they couldn't see a difference. Elvis had to prove it to them by showing the scars up in his hairline.

Even when he wasn't on the road, reporters were eager to get a "fat" quote. When Elvis checked into a Nashville motel while prepping for an ultimately abandoned recording session, the motel's staff was quoted in the paper, "The first night he ordered cheese omelets, four orders of bacon and six sweet rolls. The next thing you know he's demanding soup. No wonder his weight goes up and down like a balloon."

Of course, his eating habits weren't the only problem. Elvis was in poor health for the last years of his life, in and out of hospitals for a laundry list of problems—not the least of which was trying to decrease his dependency on prescription drugs. Although this was the era before the Betty Ford Center, Elvis was hospitalized by his primary care physician many times in an attempt to curb his bad habits.

The problem was that Elvis liked his lifestyle. He had his live-in girlfriend Linda Thompson live in at the hospital so he wouldn't be alone. He got loyal Graceland cook, Mary Jenkins, to sneak in his favorite food. Same old, same old—just in a different location.

The End Is Near

Linda Thompson was in her early twenties. At a certain point, she had to bail. Who could blame her? She put in her time. It's not surprising she went on to marry the most healthy, wholesome, physically fit man she could find: Olympic champion and Wheaties coverboy Bruce Jenner.

Meanwhile, the King of Rock and Roll's body was giving out on him. He was suffering from a whole host of illnesses that weren't going away. Upon his death, the medical examiners listed "hypertension, cardiovascular disease, atherosclerosis and coronary artery disease."

Yet the money he could still earn by going out on the road was obscene—a thirteen-day tour in 1976 reaped almost a million dollars in profit. With the overhead he had, Elvis had to keep going.

The staff dutifully trundled him onto the *Lisa Marie,* and he didn't emerge until concert time. Offstage, he wore elastic-waist sweatsuits when he wasn't wearing extralarge pajamas. The man who had once lived for looking good had clearly given up.

The Final Humiliation

In June of 1977, his management signed him up to do a CBS concert special. Less than a decade since his black-leather sex-god comeback special, only four years since his hunka-hunka burning-love satellite extravaganza, a now frighteningly feeble and fragile Elvis desperately tries to make it through his ump-teenth concert somewhere in the U.S.A. No red lights spelling Elvis in English or any other language. No trading axes with Scotty Moore or throwing capes into audiences. Just a forty-two-year-old man with a swollen face, hands, and stomach, wearing one of the few remaining jumpsuits he can fit into, struggling through the same songs he's been singing for years. His hair looks thin, his skin mottled, his eye makeup awkwardly applied. It's sad and pitiful, and to this day his estate has refused to allow it to be issued on video. No one needs to see Elvis this way.

The Final Betrayal

As hard as it is for us nowadays to believe, Elvis's private life was still private before August 1977 when, shortly before his

death, several ex-staff members published a lurid tell-all enti-
tled *"Elvis, What Happened?"*

Equally hard to believe is that Elvis didn't try harder to stop
the book from being published. True, this was in the days before it became standard operating procedure for celebrities to
have their staff members sign confidentiality agreements.

But Elvis's fatalistic acceptance of this betrayal is just another example of his "been there, done that" frame of mind.
Around the time of the book controversy, he told a friend during a phone conversation and interview that history was repeat-
ing itself. He remembered that back when he started in 1956
the media thrived on stories that "Elvis the Pelvis" was a drug
fiend and a sexual outlaw. "It broke my heart—my family's too.
But I learned not to let those things bother me too much and
though I would be disturbed at times, I refused to waste time
worrying and crying about it."

The Final Fiancée

Ginger Alden was Elvis's last official girlfriend. She was a local Memphis girl. A mutual friend introduced her and her beauty queen sister to Elvis.

The friend expected Elvis to go for the older sister, but he liked "Gingerbread" best. Ginger was only twenty when she got  sucked into Elvis's world. She had no clue what she was signing up for. Like every other Elvis girl, she probably would have abandoned ship eventually. It was Elvis who was hanging on to her like a life preserver, demanding she accompany him on tours even though she was clearly bored at the shows.

Ginger, like all of Elvis's girlfriends, has moved on. She is now happily living in obscurity as somebody else's wife.

January 1975—The dreaded forty.

February 1975—Hospitalized. "I did a three-week engagement at Baptist Hospital," he later joked onstage. "I entertained the nurses, and they entertained me!"

September 1975—Another Baptist engagement.

November 1976—Linda Thompson says sayonara. Ginger Alden signs up for active duty.

December 1976—The *Las Vegas Sun* reports Elvis is "a little heavier than he should be but not as heavy as on his previous visit."

April 1977—Back to Baptist.

August 1977—*"Elvis, What Happened?"* published. The cover blurb proclaims, "The dark other side of the brightest star in the world!"

Live Fast, Die Young

Q: What do you think about just quitting?
EP: Well, I'll put it like this—I'll never quit as long
as I'm doing okay. (1957)

lvis died hours before he was scheduled to perform in Portland, Maine. He died in his beloved Graceland. He died in one of his favorite rooms—his combined private bath and dressing room. He died surrounded by his favorite things: his clothes, mirrors, hair- and skin-care products, books, and prescription drugs. He died while his gorgeous twenty-year-old girlfriend slept in his bed in the next room. He died while his daughter played in her little princess bedroom down the hall. He died before he had to suffer the loss of his father or grandmother. He died before the CBS television special could air, showing the world what bad shape he was really in. He died when he had a hit record on the charts. He

died while he could still look relatively good in his coffin. He died on August 16, 1977. He was forty-two.

Poor Ginger Alden discovered the body. As if it wasn't enough that she had to deal with Elvis's crazy life, now she had to be the first to deal with his death.

She called down to Presley's support staff, who tried to revive their boss. Fruitless efforts continued all the way to Baptist Memorial Hospital, where nine years earlier Lisa Marie was born and where two years later Vernon Presley would die.

That afternoon the cause of death was announced: coronary arrhythmia, an irregular beating of the heart. This hurried proclamation has been seriously questioned over the years, but why bicker about what killed him? It's a miracle he stayed alive as long as he did. As Vernon explained on his son's gravestone, "God saw that he needed some rest and called him home to be with Him."

75,000 Mourners Can't Be Wrong

Although frail in health and emotionally distraught, Vernon took care of business. He dispatched Elvis's hairdresser to the funeral home. Keeping in mind Elvis's most flattering colors, he decided the King of Rock and Roll should be buried in a baby-blue shirt and a white suit from Lansky Brothers.

He then opened Graceland up for the fans to view their idol as he lay in state in the mansion's foyer. From 3 P.M. to

6:30 P.M., an estimated 75,000 people paid their last respects. Although loudspeakers announced to the crowd that no photography would be permitted inside, a picture of Elvis in his coffin would later appear on the cover of *The National Enquirer*. In that photo, Elvis looked either so good or so bad (viewer's choice) that some people refused to believe the body in the coffin was real.

I Viewed Elvis in His Coffin and Wrote About It for *Rolling Stone*

The late President Kennedy's nineteen-year-old daughter, Caroline, showed up unexpectedly at the Graceland gates after the public viewing was closed. The Presley family admitted her into their home, not realizing at first that the VIP was interning for a New York newspaper. Her article, rewritten by the *Rolling Stone* staff, was published in the issue devoted to Elvis's death.

Since very few pictures had ever been published of the interior of Graceland, Caroline was stunned by the in-your-face decorating scheme. Her article is heavy on details about the mansion's décor. Regarding Elvis, Kennedy reported that "his face seemed swollen and his sideburns reached his chin."

Ours to the End

The actual funeral service was held on the eighteenth in Graceland's living room. Among the two hundred mourners were
almost all of Elvis's ex-girlfriends, including Ann-Margret,
who couldn't stay away despite warnings that it would be a mad-
house.

Elvis was then buried at the same cemetery where he visited
his mother's grave so faithfully.

After the funeral, Vernon suggested fans each be allowed to
take a flower from the 2,200 floral arrangements sent to the
cemetery. In less than three hours, not a single petal remained.

Elvis, Go Home!

Just as Elvis couldn't have a normal life, he couldn't have a normal death. Before the month was out, three men tried to break
into his grave in a bizarre ransom scheme. Meanwhile, the fans
continued to swarm the cemetery, taking away with them anything they could scrounge up as a souvenir.

As they had done when he was alive, Elvis's "neighbors"
(people visiting others buried in the cemetery) complained that
the King of Rock and Roll's presence caused too big of a dis-
ruption. Everyone agreed it might be best if Elvis returned to
Graceland.

On October 2, 1977, Elvis's and his mother's coffins were relocated to Graceland's Meditation Garden, where they remain to this day.

Elvis Lives!

No, he doesn't. He's really dead. We can have fun with pretending he's just out there and hiding, but girls know he's really six feet under.

March 3, 1977—Signs his last will and testament, witnessed by Ginger Alden. Listed beneficiaries are daughter, Lisa Marie, grandmother Minnie Mae, and father, Vernon—in that order.

August 16, 1977—Dies. Really. There's official documentation and everything.

August 29, 1977—Three men try to steal Elvis's body from Forest Hill Cemetery.

October 3, 1977—The CBS special *Elvis in Concert* airs. At the end of the program, Vernon thanks the fans for their cards and letters.

Chapter **18**

S.W.A.K.

Girls get the final word.

> *"Please don't give people the wrong impressions of Elvis Presley. We think he's the absolute end."*
>
> JANIS OLSEN, FAN (1956)

> *"He's amazing. He's so unspoiled and fresh, everybody is crazy about him. In fact, he's more fun than a barrel of monkeys! And he is a gentleman."*
>
> DEBRA PAGET
> *Love Me Tender* COSTAR (1956)

> *"He's the most fascinating human I've ever known."*
>
> KAY WHEELER
> PRESIDENT OF THE NATION'S FIRST
> AND LARGEST ELVIS PRESLEY FAN CLUB (1957)

"He's a beautiful person."

KATY JURADO, *Stay Away, Joe*
COSTAR (1968)

"I like Tom Jones, too, but we have a saying in our house—Tom Jones is Jesus Christ, but Elvis is God Almighty."

MRS. OLGA VEGA, FAN (1972)

"Thirty of us decided to come down here [to his funeral] because there'll never be another one like him. He was the king of everyone, and especially of our people. He was the king of the gypsies. He was ours."

MYRTLE SMITH, FAN (1977)

Notes

Introduction

1 **"People are going"** "Presley Interview 1962 Part 1 & 2," *Elvis in the Beginning* CD, LaserLight Digital, 12 787, 1996. Unless noted otherwise, all attributed quotes by Elvis or Q&A with Elvis are transcriptions by the author of audio interviews and press conferences given by Presley, currently available on various compact discs or record albums.

2 **"Finally, somebody who"** e-mail from Gina Penque to www.girlsguidetoelvis, 3 February 2001.

2 **"primary buyers"** Roger Catlin, "More Elvis Releases—The Casino Recordings," *The Hartford Courant*, 15 August 2001.

3 **"survey"** *The Girls' Guide to Elvis* survey ran from July to September 2001.

8 **"I don't think many viewers"** Hal Humphrey, "Elvis Skips Gyrations but Still Generates Heat," *Los Angeles TV Times*, December 1–7, 1968, reprinted in Bill DeNight, Sharon Fox, and Ger Rijff, *Elvis Album* (New York: Beekman House, 1991), p. 222.

Chapter 1: Jon Burrows Wouldn't Smell as Sweet

11 **"Dear Mr. President"** The complete letter is on-line at the National Archives and Records Administration website.

11 **"My little daughter"** Elvis Presley, *Elvis Live in Las Vegas*, RCA, 07863 69354–2, 2001.

12 **"Jon Burrows"** Elvis provided this contact information in his letter to Nixon.

13 **"An unmarried sharecropper"** All genealogical information from Fred L. Worth and Steve D. Tamerius, *Elvis: His Life from A to Z*, (New York: Wing Books, 1992).

13 **"Aron"** "Interview with Elvis (Unreleased highlights from press conference, September 22, 1958)," *Elvis: The King of Rock 'n' Roll, The Complete 50's Masters*, Disc 4, RCA 07863 66050–2, 1992.

14 **"American Express"** Card 029 756 417 1 800 AX, issued to Elvis A. Presley. Item 70, Butterfield and Butterfield, *The Elvis Presley Museum Collection*, Vol. B40, Sale 6074B (June 18–19, 1994) (Auctioneers Corporation Catalogs, 1994), p. 11.

14 **"June 1933"** A variety of sources were consulted to create the timelines that conclude each chapter. Primary sources include Peter Guralnick and Ernst Jorgensen, *Elvis Day by Day* (New York: Ballantine Books, 1999); Worth and Tamerius, *Elvis: His Life from A to Z*; and the biographical timeline on www.elvis.com.

14 **"Jaycees program"** Item 108, Butterfield and Butterfield, *The Elvis Presley Museum Collection*, p. 20.

14 **"police department form"** Author's notes from original document, dated 9 February 1976, displayed at the Memphis Police Museum on Beale Street, August 1997.

Chapter 2: The Little Prince

17 **"Did you have a happy time"** "24 March 1956, Warwick Hotel, New York with Robert Carlton Brown," *Elvis Presley, The Interviews*, Prism Leisure, PLATCD 145, 1996.

18 **"Son, wouldn't you rather"** *Elvis Presley: His Complete Life Story in Words with More Than 100 Photos*, Prepared by the editors of *TV Radio Mirror*, 1956, p. 26.

19 **"I won fifth prize"** *Elvis Presley: The Truth about Me!—Interview—Intimate Thoughts*, Rainbow Records, 1956.

19 **"marriage license"** Item 290, Butterfield and Butterfield, *The Elvis Presley Museum Collection*, p. 55.

19 **"It was just a very sweet relationship"** Guralnick and Jorgensen, *Elvis Day by Day*, p. 7.

20 **"Elvis looked a lot like Dad"** Gladys Presley quotes from a page torn from a fan magazine, item 76, Butterfield and Butterfield, *The Elvis Presley Museum Collection*, p. 13.

20 **"Rather flashily dressed"** Notation by Miss M. Harris on form published in Guralnick and Jorgensen, *Elvis Day by Day*, p. 10.

20 **"Gladys made him quit"** *Elvis Presley . . . TV Radio Mirror*, p. 11.

21 **"Elvis didn't know how to dance"** Steve Doughtery and Linda Marx, "Elvis Prom Date Remembers a Shy Guy in Blue Suede Shoes," *People Weekly*, 17 July 1989, pp. 99–100.

21 **"He was a good kisser"** Ibid., p. 100.

22 **"Until that night"** Bill E. Burk, *Early Elvis: The Humes Years* (Memphis: Red Oak Press, 1990), p. 111.

22 **"I never was a lady killer"** Charles Manos, "Elvis Sings, Wows 15,000," *Detroit Free Press*, 26 May 1956.

22 **"I remember that when she"** *Elvis Presley . . . TV Radio Mirror*, p. 20.

22 **"It really didn't"** Interview outtakes for the documentary film *Elvis on Tour. Between Takes with Elvis*, Creative Radio and Osborne Enterprises, Inc., 1989.

24 **"pink and black"** Rose Clayton and Dick Heard, *Elvis Up Close: In the Words of Those Who Knew Him Best* (Atlanta: Turner Publishing, 1994), p. 43.

24 **"After his early"** Bernard J. Lansky, "Clothier to the King," in Guernsey's, *Elvis Presley: The Official Auction Featuring Items from the Archives of Graceland* (New York: Harry N. Abrams, Inc., 1999), p. 26.

24 **"He never wore"** Whitney Smith, "Lansky Outfitted Rock and Roll Star Throughout Career," *The Commercial Appeal*, 14 August 1987.

24 **"For his appearance on the Hayride"** Bob Masters, "Mass Hysteria: Frenzied Elvis Fans Rock Youth Center," *Shreveport Times*, 16 December 1956.

24 **"42 coat"** Lansky, "Clothier to the King," p. 29.

24 **"good eatin' "** Smith, "Lansky Outfitted Rock . . ."

Chapter 3: The Kid with the Sideburns

27 **"When you released"** "Presley Press Conference, 1961 Parts 1 & 2," *Elvis on the Road Interviews,* LaserLight Digital, 12 789, 1996. The Mr. Phillips reference is most probably addressed to Dewey Phillips, the local disc jockey who debuted Elvis's first record, and not Sam Phillips, owner of Sun Records.

27 **"I never saw"** Peter Guralnick, *Careless Love: The Unmaking of Elvis Presley* (Boston: Little, Brown and Company, 1999), p. 468.

27–28 **"Why don't you"** *Between Takes with Elvis.*

28 **"When asked"** "24 March 1956, Warwick Hotel . . . ," *Elvis Presley, The Interviews.*

28–29 **"I thought"** *Sun Days with Elvis,* exec. prod. Bob Marin, Magnum America, Inc., 1996.

29 **"sideburn business"** *Elvis Presley: The Truth about Me!*

29 **"At the first rehearsal"** Scotty Moore with James Dickerson, *That's Alright, Elvis: The Untold Story of Elvis's First Guitarist and Manager, Scotty Moore* (New York: Schirmer Books, 1997), p. 56.

30 **"kind of odd"** Ibid., p. 56.

30 **"Elvis was the only"** *Sun Days with Elvis.*

30 **"I just landed"** "Little Rock, Arkansas, May 16, 1956," *The Fifties Interviews,* Magnum Music Group, CDMF 074, 1995.

33 **"This boy has something"** "In a Spin," *Memphis Press-Scimitar,* 28 July 1954.

Chapter 4: "Girls, I'll See You Backstage"

35 **"Your actions"** *The Elvis Tapes,* Jerden Records, JRCD 7005, 1992.

36 **"*Newsweek* asked"** "Hillbilly on a Pedestal." *Newsweek,* 14 May 1956, p. 82.

36 **"He's just"** Mae Boren Axton, *Elvis Presley* (Tampa: Rinaldi Printing Company, 1978), p. 4.

36 **"He just makes me"** Lee Cotton, *Did Elvis Sing in Your Hometown?* (Sacramento, CA: High Sierra Books, 1995), p. 194.

36 **"questions of a Daytona"** "Ed Ripley Interview—1956," *The Rockin' Rebel, Vol. 3,* Golden Archives, GA 350, 1979.

37 **"One girl"** Nancy Kozikowski (née Hebenstreit), "Elvis." Unpublished personal remembrances, 1998.

38 **"Kay Wheeler"** Telephone interview with Kay Wheeler, 5 September 2001.

38 **"Q: When you get caught"** *The Elvis Tapes.*

39 **"Elvis closed the first half"** Axton, *Elvis Presley*, p. 4.

40 **"I told Elvis when"** Ibid., p. 6.

40 **"Elvis is just one out of the full list"** Kay Wheeler and William A. Harbinson, *Growing Up with the Memphis Flash* (Amsterdam, Netherlands: Tutti Frutti Productions, 1994), p. 89.

Chapter 5: A Date with Elvis

43 **"I love going out on dates"** *Elvis Presley: The Truth about Me!*

43 **"girls napping"** Caption on photograph, *The Commercial Appeal*, 23 March 1958.

44 **"You thought maybe"** Clayton and Heard, *Elvis Up Close*, p. 133.

45 **"Seventies-era girlfriend"** Andrew Hearn, "World Exclusive: Linda Thompson Talks to Essential Elvis," *Essential Elvis*, Issue 17, July–August 2001, p. 8.

45 **"Nancy recalled"** Kozikowski, "Elvis."

46 **"A fan once asked"** "Pvt. Presley answers his private mail . . . from you," *Photoplay*, November 1959.

46 **"I'm not kidding"** Peter Harry Brown and Pat Broeske, *Down at the End of Lonely Street: The Life and Death of Elvis Presley* (New York: Dutton, 1997), p. 90.

47 **"I suppose the closest"** "Elvis Sails, press interview with Elvis Presley," *Elvis Presley, The Interviews.*

48 **"Dixie Locke was fifteen"** Peter Guralnick, *Last Train to Memphis: The Rise of Elvis Presley* (Boston: Little, Brown and Company, 1994), pp. 67–87.

Chapter 6: Solid Gold

53 **"Q: Do you call it"** *Elvis Presley: The Truth about Me!*

54 **"Keep me always"** Quotes taken from original ads for Elvis products reprinted in DeNight, Fox, and Rijff, *Elvis Album*, pp. 60–2.

54 **"*Newsweek* reported"** "Presley Spells Profit." *Newsweek*, undated, Ibid., p. 60.

54 **"It's hard to believe"** Chester Morrison, "The Great Elvis Presley Industry," *Look*, 13 November 1956, p. 98.

55 **"$35 million"** Mei Fong and Debra Lau, "Earnings from the Crypt," *Forbes.com*, 28 February 2001.

56 **"Q: Did they tell you"** *Elvis Presley: The Truth about Me!*

57 **"Nobody teased"** Alanna Nash with Billy Smith, Marty Lacker, and Lamar Fike, *Elvis Aaron Presley: Revelations from the Memphis Mafia* (New York: HarperCollins, 1995), p. 95.

58 **"The Colonel asked"** E-mail correspondence with Jamie Mendoza, 26 October 2001.

59 **"blared the headline"** Frank Beckman and Carter Van Lopik, "Hysterical Shrieks Greet Elvis in His Gold Jacket and Shoes," *Detroit Free Press*, 1 April 1957.

60 RCA chronology and facts from *Elvis 56 Collector's Edition* liner notes. RCA, 07863 66817–2, 1996.

Chapter 7: There's No Place Like Home

63 **"Q: Elvis, where do you live"** *Elvis Presley: The Truth about Me!*

63 **"You got to give"** *Elvis Presley . . . TV Radio Mirror*, p. 28.

64 **"a ranch-type"** "24 March 1956, Warwick Hotel . . . ," *Elvis Presley, The Interviews*.

64 **"Elvis is always"** *Elvis Presley . . . TV Radio Mirror*, p. 28.

64 **"I Live in Elvis's House"** Telephone interview with Cindy Hazen, 9 August 2001.

66 **"At the time they purchased"** *Elvis Presley . . . TV Radio Mirror*, p. 28.

67 **"There's a famous story"** Red West, Sonny West and Dave Hebler, as told to Steve Dunleavy, *"Elvis, What Happened?"* (New York: Ballantine Books, 1977), p. 140.

67 **"I think I'm going to like"** Guralnick, *Last Train to Memphis*, p. 397.

69 **"Q: There was one story"** Jerry Osborne, *Elvis Word for Word* (New York: Harmony Books, 1999), p. 133.

70 **"Making Sense of Graceland"** Telephone interview with Karal Ann Marling, 3 August 2001.

Chapter 8: Soldier Boy

77 **"Well, I gotta go"** Alan Fortas, *Elvis—from Memphis to Hollywood: Memories from My Twelve Years with Elvis Presley* (Ann Arbor, MI: Popular Culture Ink, 1992), p. 102.

77 **"Fifteen thousand letters"** Elvis estimated he got "probably 15,000 letters a week" in a 1958 press conference, *Elvis: The King of Rock 'n' Roll, The Complete 50's Masters*, Disc 4.

78 **"Once, we found him"** Michael Hall, "Viva Fort Hood," *Texas Monthly*, December 2000, p. 203.

78 **"Elvis looked tanned"** Andrew Hearn, "Anita Wood Interview," *Essential Elvis*, reprinted in *ElvisNews.com*, 26 August 2001.

78 **"We couldn't go"** "Anita Wood Reveals—Why Elvis and I Couldn't Marry," *TV Movie Screen*, October 1958.

79 **"It was a time of grief"** Wanda June Hill, *We Remember Elvis* (Palos Verdes, CA: Morgan Press, 1978), p. 84.

80 **"I met him"** Jackson Baker, "Who Was This Woman? Who Was This Girl?" *Memphis*, July–August 1998.

81 **"To a male friend"** Fortas, *Elvis—from Memphis to Hollywood*, p. 101.

81 **"To Anita"** Osborne, *Elvis Word for Word*, p. 129.

81 **"she thought her husband"** "Anita Wood Interview," *Essential Elvis*.

81 **"Q: Elvis, what would you like"** *Elvis: The King of Rock 'n' Roll, The Complete 50's Masters*, Disc 4.

82 **"It's Grind City"** Fortas, *Elvis—from Memphis to Hollywood*, p. 102.

82 **"He's not at all conceited"** Andreas Schroer, *Private Presley, The Missing Years—Elvis in Germany.* (New York: William Morrow and Company, Inc., 1993), p. 77.

82 **"She was the last"** Priscilla Presley with Sandra Harmon, *Elvis and Me* (New York: G. P. Putnam's Sons, 1985), p. 29.

82 **"Q: Where did you spend"** "Elvis in the Army (Interview)," *The Private Presley* (CD), Morrow, 1993.

83 **"Q: What are your plans"** Ibid.

Chapter 9: Can't Help Falling in Love

87 **"Q: Are you going to keep"** *Rare Moments with the King*, Goodtimes Home Video Corporation, 1998.

88 **"The paper broke it down"** Dick Kleiner, "Mop-Haired Rivals Come and Go, but He Stays Elvis—Bigger Than Ever," *Memphis Press-Scimitar*, 12 December 1965.

90 **"worked well on television"** Guralnick, *Careless Love: The Unmaking of Elvis Presley*, p. 469.

90 **"Decoding the Elvis Films"** E-mail interview with Susan Doll, 9 September 2001.

97 **"Basically nobody dressed"** All Edith Head quotes from Edith Head and Paddy Calistro, *Edith Head's Hollywood* (New York: Dutton, 1983), pp. 120–21.

99 **"Elvis slept"** Bob Bert, "Groovin' with Nancy Sinatra," *BB Gun*, Vol. 5, 2001, p. 56.

99 **"I resented that"** Ibid., p. 56.

100 **"What we had"** Ruthe Stein, "Girls! Girls! Girls!," *San Francisco Chronicle*, 3 August 1997.

Chapter 10: Regarding Elvis's Weight

103 **"Q: Do you watch"** *Elvis in the Beginning*.

103 **"It's very important"** Guralnick and Jorgensen, *Elvis Day by Day*, p. 164.

104 **"I would get a little round"** "24 March 1956, Warwick Hotel . . . ," *Elvis Presley, The Interviews*.

105 **"His personal physician"** Clayton and Heard, *Elvis Up Close*, p. 288.

106 **"Actress Janice Pennington,"** Ibid., p. 289.

106 **"Just days"** Beth J. Tamke, "Elvis Death Report Blames Heart, Liver," *The Commercial Appeal*, 27 August 1977.

106 **"Q: Getting ready to finish"** "St. Petersburg, Florida, 7 August 1956," *The Fifties Interviews*.

106 **"His girlfriend, Dixie"** "Sun's Newest Star: Elvis Presley," reprinted in Ger Rijff, *Long Lonely Highway: A 1950's Elvis Scrapbook* (Ann Arbor, MI: Pierian Press, 1985, 1987), p. 59.

107 **"gigantic"** Presley with Harmon, *Elvis and Me*, p. 29.

107 **"He didn't like chicken"** "Meals Fit for the King," *People Weekly*, 19 June 2000, p. 117.

107 **"When you calculate"** All calorie and fat-gram counts calculated by Bear Fisher.

107 **"How to Eat Like Elvis"** All calorie and fat-gram counts for "The Elvis way" (except where noted) are based on recipes published in Mary Jenkins (as told to Beth Pease), *Memories Beyond Graceland Gates* (Buena Park, CA: West Coast Publishing, 1989). The *Girls' Guide to Elvis* way recipes created by the author and Bear Fisher on 26 September 2001.

112 **"he'd inhale three at a time"** "Meals Fit for the King," *People Weekly*, p. 117.

113 **"Pork Chops and Okra"** Based on recipes published in Lucy Hanley, ed., *Elvis' Greatest Hits . . . Recipes and More from Graceland* (Westlake Village, CA: John Hinde Curteich, Inc., 2001).

113 **"He raved about"** "Nick Adams," *Elvis—A Golden Celebration*, RCA, CPM6–5172, 1984.

114 **"If he wanted them"** *The Burger and the King: The Life and Cuisine of Elvis Presley*, Dir. James Marsh, Arena/BBC, 1995.

116 **"Pound Cake with Peaches and Cream"** Personal interview with Sandi Miller, 28 September 2001.

117 **"Writes 150 pounds"** Guralnick and Jorgensen, *Elvis Day by Day*, p. 10.

117 **"*Variety* reports"** Lee Cotton, *Did Elvis Sing in Your Hometown, Too?* (Sacramento, CA: High Sierra Books, 1997), p. 103.

Chapter 11: Perfect Hair

119 **"I stopped using"** "1972, Elvis's New York Press Conference Before his Madison Square Garden Show," *Elvis Presley, The Interviews*.

119 **"Hal Wallis wrote a memo"** Guralnick and Jorgensen, *Elvis Day by Day*, p. 192.

120 **"Only his hairdresser"** Telephone interview with Larry Geller, 13 August 2001.

Chapter 12: Being Mrs. Presley

129 **"Q. If you found someone"** "Elvis Sails, press interview with Elvis Presley," *Elvis Presley, The Interviews*.

129 **"Jerry Lee Lewis"** Jerry Lee Lewis married thirteen-year-old Myra Gale Brown on 12 December 1957. Loretta Lynn, who was born the same year as Elvis, was thirteen when she first met her husband, Mooney.

129 **"romancing the underaged"** Presley with Harmon, *Elvis and Me*, p. 58. Nash et al., *Elvis Aaron Presley: Revelations from the Memphis Mafia*, p. 204.

130 **"Sharon Purkey Fields"** "Celebrity Classmates: Priscilla Presley Hid Elvis' Love from her School Pals," *The National Enquirer*, 4 June 2001, p. 14.

130 **"Everyone knew"** Telephone interview with Rona Barrett, 7 September 2001.

130 **"By the time"** Brown and Broeske, *Down at the End of Lonely Street,* pp. 317–18.

131 **"According to Priscilla"** Sheila Weller, "Priscilla Presley: Surviving Elvis," *McCall's,* May 1979, p. 20.

131 **"Everybody was trying to figure"** Barrett telephone interview.

131 **"Then"** Thomas F. BeVier, "Wedding Is Typically Elvis—Quick, Quiet and in Style," *The Commercial Appeal,* 2 May 1967.

133 **"Sometimes I think if"** Weller, "Priscilla Presley: Surviving Elvis," p. 173.

133 **"Priscilla was very meek"** Telephone interview with Sandi Miller, 7 September 2001.

134 **"hot sex"** Presley with Harmon, *Elvis and Me,* p. 297. Suzanne Finstad, *Child Bride: The Untold Story of Priscilla Beaulieu Presley* (New York: Harmony Books, 1997), pp. 236–39. Nash et al., *Elvis Aaron Presley: Revelations from the Memphis Mafia,* p. 626.

134 **"Certainly she has done"** Suzanne Andrews, "Making Elvis Pay," *Working Woman,* September 1993, p. 99.

135 **"It was no big romance"** Videotape of the press conference held in Vernon's office at Graceland now shown on the Graceland tour.

Chapter 13: Sex with Elvis

137 **"EP: You know that girl"** *This Is Elvis* (theatrical version). Written, produced, and directed by Andrew Solt and Malcolm Leo, Warner Bros., 1981.

138 **"on the slight side"** Suzanne Finstad, *Child Bride: The Untold Story of Priscilla Beaulieu Presley* (New York: Harmony Books, 1997), p. 95.

138 **"He was not hung"** Peter Whitmer, Ph.D., *The Inner Elvis: A Psychological Biography of Elvis Aaron Presley* (New York: Hyperion Press, 1996), p. 341.

138 **"An army buddy"** Joe Esposito and Elena Oumano, *Good Rockin' Tonight: Twenty Years on the Road and on the Town with Elvis* (New York: Simon and Schuster, 1994), p. 38.

138 **"I remember the first time"** Finstad, *Child Bride,* p. 184.

138 **"He liked certain things"** Esposito and Oumano, *Good Rockin' Tonight,* p. 191.

139 **"He was a classic voyeur"** Brown and Broeske, *Down at the End of Lonely Street*, p. 264.

139 **"Elvis was particularly"** Esposito and Oumano, *Good Rockin' Tonight*, p. 187.

139 **"He had a thing"** Red West, Sonny West, and Dave Hebler, as told to Steve Dunleavy, *"Elvis, What Happened?"* (New York: Ballantine Books, 1977), p. 282.

139 **"Priscilla found"** Presley with Harmon, *Elvis and Me*, p. 259.

140 **"a gentle, considerate"** "Love Him Tenderly," *People Weekly*, 18 August 1997, p. 85.

140 **"abortion"** Joyce Bova, as told to William Conrad Nowels, *Don't Ask Forever: My Love Affair with Elvis: A Washington Woman's Secret Years with Elvis Presley* (New York: Kensington Books, 1994), pp. 238–40.

140 **"I found it to be"** Whitmer, *The Inner Elvis*, p. 415.

140 **"We all have our preferences"** Baker, "Who Was This Woman? Who Was This Girl?"

Chapter 14: The Comeback

143 **"Q: For many years"** *Rare Moments with the King*.

143 **"He was worried"** Sandi Miller telephone interview.

144 **"More women"** Ad reprinted in Robert Gordon, *The King on the Road: Elvis on Tour, 1954–1977* (New York: St. Martin's Press, 1996), p. 144.

144 **"He may have worn"** Mike Thomas, "Bill Belew, the Man Who Dressed the King," *Salon.com*, 18 December 1999.

145 **"Q: Is your stage"** *Rare Moments with the King*.

146 **"When Elvis was in"** Clayton and Heard, *Elvis Up Close*, p. 245.

146 **"His music"** Ibid., p. 248.

147 **"When people went to see"** Ibid., p. 263.

148 **"a white Batman"** Cotton, *Did Elvis Sing in Your Hometown, Too?*, p. 75.

148 **"Elvis admitted"** In his Jaycees award acceptance speech.

149 **"$65,000"** "The Great Bill Belew Interview," published on *Elvisnews.com* in Week 35, 2000.

149 **"Manned with giant"** "Remembering the King," *People Weekly*, 21 August 1989.

149 **"the audience thought"** *Between Takes with Elvis*.

150 **"Don't be so rough"** *Having Fun with Elvis, Vol. IV*, HK, 1970–2000 EP-4, 2000.

151 **"There were people"** Telephone interview with Robin Rosaaen, 19 September 2001.

152 **"Honey, I love you too"** Cotton, *Did Elvis Sing in Your Hometown, Too?*, p. 114.

152 **"You couldn't take your"** Robin Rosaaen interview.

152 **"Elvis was on"** Cotton, *Did Elvis Sing in Your Hometown, Too?*, p. 198.

153 **"Husbands still"** Ibid., p. 75.

Chapter 15: La Vida Loca

157 **"They're gonna"** Elvis Presley, *On Stage—February 1970*, RCA, LSP–4362, 1970.

158 **"I would love"** Elvis's original handwritten letter to Nixon is part of the National Archives.

158 **"tight-fitting"** Egil "Bud" Krogh, *The Day Elvis Met Nixon* (Bellevue, WA: Pejama Press, 1994), p. 18.

160 **"open marriage"** Guralnick, *Careless Love*, p. 396.

160 **"separated"** Michael Lollar, "Woman with Elvis No Longer a Mystery," *The Commercial Appeal*, 8 January 2000.

160 **"By the time"** "Women Shaped the Kingdom," *The Commercial Appeal*, 14 August 1987, p. EP19.

161 **"It's unusual"** Jerry Hopkins, *Elvis: The Final Years* (New York: St. Martin's Press, 1980), p. 180.

161 **"Elvis knew"** Clayton and Heard, *Elvis Up Close*, p. 253.

161 **"You don't expect"** "Elvis' Whim Caters to Car Shopper's Fancy," *The Commercial Appeal*, 29 July 1975.

Chapter 16: Fat and Forty

167 **"EP: When we're not"** "24 March 1956, Warwick Hotel" *Elvis Presley, The Interviews.*

167 **"middle-age spread"** "Presley Does a Split, Leaves Crowd Panting," 2 January 1976, reprinted in DeNight, Fox, and Rijff, *Elvis Album*, p. 274.

167 **"Not only"** "A Fat Elvis Can Still Make Female Fans Squeal," Ibid., p. 275.

167 **"Elvis is fat, and there's no"** "Fat and Forty—But Also Sold Out," *Memphis Press-Scimitar*, 7 September 1976.

168 **"Several of his staff"** Hopkins, *Elvis: The Final Years*, p. 185.
168 **"The first night"** "Elvis Presley No-Shows RCA Recording Session," *Memphis Press-Scimitar*, 2 February 1977.
169 **"hospitalized"** Guralnick and Jorgensen, *Elvis Day by Day*, p. 346. Brown and Broeske reported that "drug detoxification" was listed on Elvis's hospital forms. Brown and Pat Broeske, *Down at the End of Lonely Street*, p. 392.
169 **"hypertension"** Beth J. Tamke, "Elvis Death Report Blames Heart, Liver," *The Commercial Appeal*, 27 August 1977.
169 **"almost a million"** Guralnick and Jorgensen, *Elvis Day by Day*, p. 364.
171 **"It broke"** Hill, *We Remember Elvis*, p. 90.
173 **"I did a three-week"** *Having Fun with Elvis on Stage*, Vol. IV.
173 **"a little heavier"** Joe Delaney, "Joe Delaney Column," *Las Vegas Sun*, 5 December 1976.

Chapter 17: Live Fast, Die Young

175 **"Q: What do you think"** *The Elvis Tapes*.
175 **"hit record"** "Way Down"/"Pledging My Love" shipped on June 6. Guralnick and Jorgensen, *Elvis Day by Day*, p. 376.
176 **"cause of death"** William Steverson, "Final Glimpse of Fallen Star Lures Faithful," *The Commercial Appeal*, 18 August 1977.
177 **"The late President"** Caroline Kennedy, "Graceland," *Rolling Stone*, 22 September 1977, p. 40.
177 **"showed up unexpectedly"** Guralnick, *Careless Love*, p. 656. Brown and Pat Broeske, *Down at the End of Lonely Street*, p. 423.
177 **"rewritten"** Robert Draper, *Rolling Stone Magazine: The Uncensored History* (New York: Doubleday, 1990), p. 268.
177 **"his face"** Kennedy, "Graceland," p. 40.
178 **"2,200 floral arrangements"** "Wailing Elvis Fans to Receive Flowers," *UPI*, 19 Friday 1977.

Chapter 18: S.W.A.K.

183 **"Please don't"** "Letters to the Editor," *Life*, 17 September 1956.
183 **"He's amazing"** "Elvis Presley Becomes a Movie Star," reprinted in DeNight, Fox, and Rijff, *Elvis Album*, p. 70.
183 **"He's the most fascinating"** Masters, "Mass Hysteria . . ."

184 **"He's a beautiful"** "The New Elvis," reprinted in DeNight, Fox, and Rijff, *Elvis Album,* p. 218.

184 **"I like Tom Jones"** Grace Lichtenstein, "Presley Draws 2 Generations of Fans," *New York Times,* 10 June 1972.

184 **"Thirty of us"** Chet Flippo, "In Memphis," *Rolling Stone,* 22 September 1977, p. 40.

Photo and illustration credits:

ii   *The Commercial Appeal*

x   Publicity still from *Jailhouse Rock,* An Avon Production/An M-G-M Release, copyright 1957 by Loew's Incorporated.

2   Record cover reproduced by kind permission of the RCA Records Label, a unit of BMG Entertainment. All rights reserved.

3   Publicity still from *Blue Hawaii,* A Hal Wallis Production/A Paramount Picture, copyright 1961 by Hal B. Hallis and Joseph H. Hazen.

4   Keith Alverson, P. O. Box 1666, Palmetto, GA 30268

5   James R. Reid

6   Publicity still from the *'68 Comeback Special,* Michael Ochs Archives.com.

7   Don Cravens, TimePix

8   James R. Reid

10   Record cover reproduced by kind permission of the RCA Records Label, a unit of BMG Entertainment. All rights reserved.

16   Record cover reproduced by kind permission of the RCA Records Label, a unit of BMG Entertainment. All rights reserved.

21   Debra Lex, TimePix

23   Original costume illustration by Kevin Ackerman

26   Record cover reproduced by kind permission of the RCA Records Label, a unit of BMG Entertainment. All rights reserved.

32   Record cover reproduced by kind permission of the RCA Records Label, a unit of BMG Entertainment. All rights reserved.

34   Robert W. Kelley, TimePix

37   Courtesy of Nancy Kozikowski

39   Robert Williams, *The Commercial Appeal*

42   Publicity still from *Loving You,* A Hal Wallis Production/A Paramount Picture, Copyright 1957 by Paramount Pictures Corporation.

44   *The Commercial Appeal*

45 Courtesy of Nancy Kozikowski
47 Michael Ochs Archives.com
48 Michael Ochs Archives.com
52 Tom Barber, *The Commercial Appeal*
56 The Library of Congress, LC–USZ62–114912
57 Publicity still from *Love Me Tender,* Copyright 1956, Twentieth Century-Fox Corp.
57 Record cover reproduced by kind permission of the RCA Records Label, a unit of BMG Entertainment. All rights reserved.
58 Kevin Ackerman
59 Courtesy of Jamie Mendoza, Nudie's Custom Java
62 *The Commercial Appeal*
66 Don Cravens, TimePix
69 *The Commercial Appeal*
73 Jeff Payne
76 Record cover reproduced by kind permission of the RCA Records Label, a unit of BMG Entertainment. All rights reserved.
80 James Whitmore, TimePix
83 James R. Reid
86 Publicity still from *Blue Hawaii,* A Hal Wallis Production/A Paramount Picture, copyright 1961 by Hal B. Hallis and Joseph H. Hazen.
89 Publicity still from *Blue Hawaii,* A Hall Wallis Production/A Paramount Picture, copyright 1961 by Hal B. Hallis and Joseph H. Hazen.
93 Publicity still from *Viva Las Vegas,* An M-G-M Picture, Copyright 1964 by Metro-Goldwyn-Mayer, Inc.
97 Kevin Ackerman
99 Michael Ochs Archives.com
102 James R. Reid
105 James R. Reid
118 Publicity still from *Viva Las Vegas,* An M-G-M Picture, Copyright 1964 by Metro-Goldwyn-Mayer, Inc.
128 Frank Edwards, TimePix
133 James R. Reid
136 Publicity still from *Jailhouse Rock,* An Avon Production/An M-G-M Release, copyright 1957 by Loew's Incorporated.
142 Record cover reproduced by kind permission of the RCA Records Label, a unit of BMG Entertainment. All rights reserved.
144 Kevin Ackerman

145   Keith Alverson

147   Kevin Ackerman

148   Elvis and Elvis Presley are registered trademarks with the USPTO,
Elvis Presley Enterprises, Inc. Doll manufactured by Mattel, Inc.
Used with permission.

149   Sandi Miller

150   Keith Alverson

151   James R. Reid

152   Keith Alverson

153   Keith Alverson

156   Dave Darnell, *The Commercial Appeal*

158   Ollie Atkins, National Archives and Records Administration

159   Ollie Atkins, National Archives and Record Administration

159   National Archives and Records Administration

160   James R. Reid

163   Record insert reproduced by kind permission of the RCA Records
Label, a unit of BMG Entertainment. All rights reserved.

163   Photo courtesy of BMG Entertainment Archives.

163   Photo courtesy of BMG Entertainment Archives.

166   Keith Alverson

172   Keith Alverson

174   Robb Mitchell, *The Commercial Appeal*

179   Kim Adelman

182   Robert Williams, *The Commercial Appeal*

186   Publicity still from *Jailhouse Rock,* An Avon Production/An M-G-M
Release, copyright 1957 by Loew's Incorporated.

Acknowledgments

The author wishes to thank (in alphabetical order):

Sylvia Abumuhor

Kevin Ackerman

Molly-Dodd Wheeler Adams

Craig Adelman

Howard Adelman

Nancy Adelman

Lorraine Alkire

Keith Alverson

Shirley Anderson

Betsy Areddy

Helen Ashford

John Bakke

Rona Barrett

Bill Belew

David Birdsell

Lisa Bostic

Chava Boylan

Pat H. Broeske

Maria Burton

John Cacciatore

Matt Cartsonis

Susan Cartsonis

Tracy Chaput

William Clark

Becky Cole

Maria de la Torre

Beth Dickey

Leslie Dinaberg

Susan Doll

Stacy Eanes

Noah Edelson

Debbie Felton

Bear Fisher

Brenda Friend

Larry Geller

Peter Guralnick

Michael Hall

Betty Harper

Cindy Hazen

Kelly Hill

Terri Hughes

Andre Jacquemetton

Maria Jacquemetton

Deb Jarnes

Claire Johnson

Claude Jones

Sara Juarez

Amy Jurist

Pei Koay

Zak Klobucher

Nancy Kozikowski

Gwendolyn A. Lewis

Holly Mandel

Karal Ann Marling

Carol May

Jeff McAdory

David McGee

Jamie Mendoza

Andrew Mersmann

Joel Metzger

Ron Milbauer

Loren Miller

Sandi Miller

Louise Neibold

Sandra Neufeldt

Suzanne Oaks

John O'Hara

Michael Omansky

Lynn Padilla

Jeff Payne

Bob Pederson

Gina Penque

Catherine Pollock

Doris Quon

Jim Reid

Ron Romain

Robin Rosaaen

Ralph Sall

Jessica Sands

Mara Schwartz

Roger Semon

Kimberly Sharp

Katie Shiban

Tricia Stewart Shiu

Lesley Marlene Siegel

Sarah Stanley

Linda Steinman

Jonathon Sterns

Cathy Tanzer

Rona Tuccillo

Peggy Van Norman

Craig Wells

Kay Wheeler

Sue Wiegert

Wendy Wilson

Alison Winward

Index

Page numbers of illustrations appear in italics.

Carol Sheridan

About the Author

Kim Adelman, a second-generation Elvis fan, is the founder of GirlsGuidetoElvis.com. She is also a filmmaker whose credits include *Why Liberace, George Lucas at USC,* and nineteen other short films. Her work has premiered at Robert Redford's prestigious Sundance Film Festival. Adelman lives in Los Angeles.